THE MARCH RETREAT

THE
MARCH RETREAT

BY

GENERAL SIR HUBERT GOUGH
G.C.M.G., K.C.B., K.C.V.O., etc.

CASSELL
and Company, Ltd.
London, Toronto, Melbourne
and Sidney

First published 1934

Printed in Great Britain by Butler & Tanner Ltd., Frome and London
F30.934

PREFACE

IN " The Fifth Army " I have told in considerable detail the story of that army. It is
inevitably a long book and necessarily the published price is high. It has always been a matter
of regret to me that the price placed it out of
reach of so many of those soldiers who served
under my command and the friends and relations
of those who died fighting in the ranks of the
Fifth Army. To reprint the whole book and issue
it at a low price is impossible and so I am falling
in with the suggestion that has often been made to
me to reprint that part of the work which deals
with the Fifth Army's crowning achievement,
popularly known as " The March Retreat."
Although the Fifth Army was nearly destroyed,
it fulfilled its rôle, it carried out its task. In their
broad outline the dispositions of the Commander-
in-Chief were suited and proper to meet the
situation which faced him, although Mr. Lloyd
George will never be able to justify keeping back
such large numbers of reinforcements as he had
at his disposal in England, and this, in spite of
the fact that he is a master of self-justification.
    Thus it arose that the Fifth Army was left with

a most dangerously thin line to face the great cyclone which all knew was coming. It was necessary for the supreme command to gain time, to safeguard the Channel Ports, to husband its resources and to exhaust the enemies' strength, and this terribly difficult rôle was given to the Fifth Army.

The German Army, on the other hand, knew that this was their last throw, and every resource which great generalship and great soldiers were capable of was called in to ensure a decisive and final victory. By what splendid, almost super-human efforts, with what long-enduring heroism and steadfastness, the officers and men of the Fifth Army stemmed that great flood, tore hope and faith from the resolute hearts of the German soldiers and eventually left them as exhausted as ourselves, are related in these pages.

The British Commander-in-Chief meanwhile had economized his forces and with many divisions in hand was able to make the great counter-stroke some months later which resulted in victory for the Allies. As the late Lord Birkenhead said in his book, " Turning Points of History," as a result of the triumph in retreat of the Fifth Army " Amiens was saved ; so was Paris ; so were the Channel Ports. So was France. So was England."

CONTENTS

I

THE APPROACH OF THE STORM

I

THE APPROACH OF THE STORM

The Fifth Army moves South—Signs of the Coming Attack
—Preparations for Defence—The Immensity of the
Task—The German Concentration—The Days before
the Battle.

I [1]

HAIG had decided to bring the Battles of
Ypres to a close. The Fifth Army was
once again withdrawn, to be launched into
another maelstrom, fiercer and more desperate
than any which it had as yet encountered.

By the 2nd of November 1917, we handed the
area of the II Corps back to the Second Army.
This Army made another attack on Passchendaele on November 6, in which we took no part
beyond supporting it with our artillery, and on
November 14 our Head-quarters in the north
closed and we opened at Dury, south of Amiens,
where we remained about a month in G.H.Q.
Reserve.

During this period of waiting, Byng brought off
his successful surprise with tanks in the direction
of Cambrai, capturing about 100 German guns.

[1] See Sketch Map 1, facing p. 18.

I was on leave at the time and this success caused immense excitement and rejoicings at home. For the first time in the war bells were rung all over the country. But the enemy command was not long in striking back, and within a few days the Germans attacked Byng at his weakest spot, captured 100 guns from him, and inflicted heavy casualties on his troops.

As a surprise Byng's attack was brilliantly executed. It might indeed have produced even greater results, and Cambrai itself could have been captured. Nevertheless, there were not sufficient troops at hand to gain any decisive results, and some critics are inclined to think that it was, in consequence, a wasted effort, but the constant demands of the French for activity on our part cannot be overlooked, and this was but one more incident in the long-drawn British effort.

No definite orders about the future of the Fifth Army were at first given to its Staff, but by the end of November we were able to make a good guess that our destination was the French front on the right of the Third Army. Up to date this had been a quiet sector and was lightly held by two French corps only ; but though quiet at the moment, it was a considerable addition to the British front—about twenty-eight miles—to which Haig very naturally objected and against which he strongly protested.

The French argument was that the share of the front to be held by them and the British

4

should be calculated principally on the mileage of the total front. Strategical reasons were not considered ; the vital importance of the Channel Ports to Great Britain in general and the British Army in particular was overlooked, and the strength of the German Army opposite the British as compared to its strength on the French front received little or no consideration : nor did the fact that serious fighting was impossible on more than half of the front of the French Army—in the semi-mountainous country of the Vosges, behind which lay the great fortresses.

Our Mission at French G.Q.G., however, strongly espoused the French view, and Lloyd George and his Cabinet having more confidence in the French Command than in Haig, the latter's protests were over-ridden and we eventually had to take over the whole of this great increase of front. The results which quickly followed placed the British Army in the greatest peril, at the same time thoroughly shaking the confidence and nerve of the Cabinet at home when it awoke by the end of March to the full consequences of its own decision.

By the 13th of December we found ourselves at Dec. 13. Villers-Bretonneux, and the Fifth Army, instead of taking over at once from the French, was directed to take over the VII Corps and the Cavalry Corps on the right of the Third Army. This gave the Fifth Army a front of about twelve miles to begin with, down to the Omignon River,

with the 16th, 21st and 9th Divisions on the VII
Corps front, under General Sir T. Snow on the
left, and five cavalry divisions and the 24th
Division on the Cavalry Corps front, under Sir
Charles Kavanagh on the right.

I found on taking over my new front that the
enemy was active in making raids and took a
prisoner or two from us regularly, several nights
a week, and this was the first sign which came
to my notice that our front was likely to be the
one selected for attack by the Germans.

The trench system was in a very neglected
state. On some parts of the front there was no
continuous line, no dugouts or observation posts,
and communication trenches were few and provided inadequate cover.

Administratively, especially to the south towards Barisis, the area was very awkward. It
had naturally been organized to receive from and
to deliver towards Paris. It had now to face
towards the British centres of activity, a change
which caused much thought and constructive
work to those concerned.

During 1917 the policy of the British Army had
been entirely offensive, and all its resources in
engineers, material, etc., had been devoted to
dealing with this side of the operations. Defensive measures, therefore, had been much neglected.

On the first day that I drove out of my Head-
quarters to go to the front, I saw to my surprise
parties of French civilians busy filling in trenches

6

and removing wire along a line which ran about a mile on the east of the village of Villers-Bretonneux. This line was part of the defences of Amiens, which had been elaborately constructed and heavily wired nearly two years previously and were still in an excellent state. The agricultural population, however, was anxious to bring all this land back into cultivation, and its appeals had been yielded to. The choice of the moment for granting this concession was ill-advised, for the collapse of Russia had made the prospect of a great German attack almost a certainty, and it was no time for demolishing good defences. Almost my first act, therefore, on taking over this sector was to stop all further demolition of this line, and to commence its reconstruction. It was well I did so, for it was on this line that "Carey's Force" stood—the last reserve scraped together by the Fifth Army for the defence of the battle front at the end of March 1918.

By December 17 very full and detailed instructions were issued for the organization of our line defensively, and for the conduct of the troops in case of attack, and the next day the Army Staff had a conference which dealt with the improvement and increase of trenches, railways, bridges, roads and organization of the necessary labour. There was a great deal which required attention and work—and with the weak divisions and extended fronts it was very difficult to provide sufficient labour for everything.

7

Telephone lines on this front had not been buried, and it was estimated that it would now require 500 men working continuously, two or three months, to carry out this important work properly.

The result of a week's inspection and study of our new front was the issue of a considerable number of orders and instructions which covered a wide field in the matter of defence. The general policy which I laid down for the Army was to reduce the front to quiet and, as far as possible, to withdraw some of the men and guns for rest and training, and to concentrate all our energies on improving our very poor defences.

It was now that Neill Malcolm was taken from me and sent to command a division. His departure was a serious loss to the Fifth Army at such a moment, when we were taking over a new task of the utmost gravity. Malcolm went off to command the 66th Division, composed of men from Manchester, and within a few weeks he returned to the Fifth Army with his new command to carry on in another sphere some splendid work in the struggle which even then was looming before us. This division, though a comparatively new one, was animated by a great spirit of comradeship, cheerfulness, and *esprit de corps* which stood it in good stead in the coming battle, and enabled it to hold together, heroically carrying on the fight, even after a week of that

8

desperate storm which reduced the divisions to mere skeletons.

In place of Malcolm I asked G.H.Q. for Brig.-General Samuel Wilson, as I knew him and appreciated his worth. He had not only worked under me at the Staff College prior to the war, but had also been through two great battles with the Fifth Army as B.G.G.S. to General Jacob in the II Corps.

G.H.Q. refused this request and Major-General Percy was sent to me, though as a Staff Officer he was an entire stranger to me. However, he responded well to the heavy call which was made on him, though on principle G.H.Q. was, in my view, wrong in not acceding to my request.

At the same time my Deputy Quartermaster-General was changed, and Major-General Percy Hambro became responsible for the administration of the Army. His work in this important capacity was quite invaluable. No man could have had a more difficult or strenuous task. A vast amount of new organization covering every form of administration had to be built up prior to the battle. This was not confined to the requirements for fighting on the Army front—a study large enough by itself—but arrangements had also to be made for a possible retreat—getting away hospitals, sick, wounded, stores of all kinds, prisoners, and the units of the Labour Corps. Hambro held a weekly conference with the Staff Officers of the four Corps concerned in these matters, kept in close touch with them, went into all their difficulties with them, and eventually when the testing time came, he was able to get away most of our " impedimenta " without undue hitches. There can be few examples in history of the administration services so successfully carrying out their job in the course of a retreat of such magnitude and under such desperate conditions. Hambro's ability, thoroughness, tact, and above all his calm, placid grin, were invaluable assets to the Fifth Army in March.

Jan. 14.   By January 14 we had taken over another Corps front, this time from the French III Corps. The XVIII Corps came in here and thus Maxse also returned to me to help in conducting another great battle. His line stretched to a point just south of St. Quentin—a further extension of twelve miles to the Army front.

Jan. 30.   By the 30th of January we took over yet a further eighteen miles of front : this carried our line beyond the Oise, as far as Barisis, making a total front of forty-two miles.

This portion was occupied by the III Corps under Sir W. Pulteney. On this great front of forty-two miles I had at first only eight divisions, with the equivalent of another in the Cavalry Corps, and with no supports or reserves whatever. A part of this new front was supposed to be defended by the Oise, but we were now having a spell of frost and dry weather, with an occasional snow-storm, and already the marshes and the river showed signs of drying up to an extent which considerably lessened the value of the river as either a defence or an obstacle. Even as early as February we were able, on several occasions, to push patrols across to the far bank of the river.

On the new front taken over from the French, the front-line defences were good, but nothing existed in rear beyond a good line of wire ; but to defend this neither trenches nor dugouts existed. Urgent orders were issued for units to get on with the work with the few resources at our disposal. A Battle Zone consisting of front line, support and reserve trenches, with the many necessary dugouts, communicating trenches, and " switches " had to be constructed, and behind that a " Green Line " or Rear Zone, both lines running along the whole forty-two miles of our front.

On February 9, in replying to a letter of the Feb. 9. 1st of February from me (to which I refer later), G.H.Q. ordered me to prepare the defences of the Péronne bridge-head—a line of about twenty-five miles in extent—and behind that again the line of the Somme and the Tortille, another twenty-five miles. To complete all these defences with support and reserve lines and supporting redoubts entailed digging about 300 miles of actual trenches and erecting the necessary wiring —a stupendous amount of fortification. The amount of labour and material required for the completion of these schemes would have been enormous, but even if it had all been available on the spot—which was far from being the case —time also was required for the work. No amount of labour—nothing short of a fairy wand —could have prepared all those defences in a few weeks ; it was a question of months, especially as little had been done in the way of defences during the previous year. Unfortunately the Fifth Army was to be called on to pay the penalty for this neglect by the previous commands before it took over in December 1917—not only in meeting the storm with the inevitable losses, for which it was prepared, but also subsequently in bearing for many years all the criticism and odium for such neglect for which it was in no way responsible.

Correspondence with G.H.Q. eventually produced an army of labour amounting to 68,000 men, but a large proportion of these did not arrive till March and they were not able to do much in the week or two at their disposal before the attack fell upon us.

This Labour Corps was so organized by my Chief Engineer, Major-General P. G. Grant, that every man had a day's rest once a week and we could count only on 48,000, or a little more than 1,000 per mile of front, after deductions for men sick or on leave. Its work consisted of making railways, roads, bridges, preparing sidings, platforms and dumps of ammunition, huts, aerodromes, etc., in addition to the defences.

On 30th December the Labour Corps strength
was about . . . . 17,400 men.
On 27th January . . . 21,000 „
On 23rd February . . . 37,800 „
On 9th March . . . 48,000 „

Of these, on 9th March, about 7,000 were
prisoners of war, who were not permitted to
work in the forward areas.

    18,000 British (Labour Battalions).
    3,000 Indians.
    4,000 Chinese.
and 7,500 Italians.

On the 16th of March, five days before the
battle, the labour in the Army was distributed
as follows :

About 10,000 men were employed on roads,
  „   4,500   .   .   .   railways,
  „   7,000   .   .   .   depots,
                                   dumps, etc.,
  „   3,500   .   .   .   hutments,
and after meeting other calls and allowing for
sickness, etc., there were less than 9,000 available
for defences, the responsibility for which had to
be undertaken principally by the few troops
available.

In early January there were only 165 men
available for work on defences, early in February
only 625, and in the middle of that month, 2,400.

My first week or so was occupied in trying to
see as much of my wide front as I could, and to get
some idea of its features, tactical characteristics,

and the general defensive organization. I then paid a visit to General Humbert of the Third French Army, whom I had just relieved, in order to get his views of the ground and the problem generally, which he knew very well, having held this sector for a long period. He told me that the Germans were certainly preparing an attack in front of us, but he was then not sure whether they would use their central position to attack southwards against the French, or westwards against us. Talking of our forward position on the high ground south of St. Quentin, he said : " *on peut vous donner un vilain coup* "—and pointed out that the Germans could drive us back into and over the Crozat Canal which passed behind our right at a distance of about four to seven miles. This visit was shortly followed by another to General Pétain at French G.Q.G. The French Staff was installed in Compiègne and I spent a night there. General Anthoine was now Chief of the Staff to Pétain : he and I were excellent friends as the result of our acquaintance and co-operation in the battles round Ypres the previous autumn. I spent most of my time at Compiègne in his office, discussing the general situation and the arrangements for French reinforcements to come up behind my right in case of necessity. It should be explained here that Haig had made it a condition of his taking over the extra thirty miles of French front—that though he would hold it with British troops, he could spare no supports to help the battle there, if such became necessary. These must be supplied by the French. The number and proximity of these divisions became therefore a matter of considerable interest to me and the Fifth Army. The question of command and supply would be difficult and would be bound to be unsatisfactory, but these conditions had to be accepted in the circumstances.

When Mr. Lloyd George forced Haig to take over this extra front, he never considered these difficulties. Yet when the time came their influence, if not decisive, was at the least very adverse to the conduct of the battle, and created some dangerous situations.

I understood at this time that General Humbert of the Third French Army, with six to eight divisions which we had relieved, would remain in the vicinity of Clermont and Compiègne and therefore close and convenient to us. It was part of the bargain with Haig on his agreeing to take over this extension of front from the French that, as soon as these divisions should arrive on the battle front, the French were to reassume responsibility for this part of the line.

As things turned out, the various threats and rumours set on foot by the German High Command so deceived Pétain that notwithstanding his previous understanding with Haig most of these divisions were moved away, some behind Rheims, some behind Verdun, and some even to the extreme right near the Swiss frontier. The result was that the agreed reserves were not able to come into line as expected and only arrived after considerable delays, without proper Staff, transport or artillery, and with inadequate supplies of ammunition—in some cases only 50 rounds per man. It was during this visit that the French Staff gave me a pamphlet it had prepared on the German organization and preparations for the battles of Riga and Caporetto, and I discussed with them the similarities of the situation which now existed on the Fifth Army's front. I had just learned that Von Hutier had appeared opposite us in command of the German Eighteenth Army. Except for a short period in command of a Guard division in France in 1914, his service had been continuously on the Russian front, where he had been responsible for many large-scale and highly-successful attacks. The fact of his presence now on my front seemed to portend that something of a similar nature to these battles was to be attempted.

This valuable piece of knowledge reached us in a curious way, which is worth relating as an example of the difficulty of maintaining complete secrecy in war.

A young German airman had been shot down and died in our lines and we learnt his name and the location of his aerodrome. A few weeks afterwards there was published in an obscure Baden newspaper a letter signed by Von Hutier,

16

addressed to the mother of this airman, express-
ing his sorrow at the loss of her gallant boy.
This paper came into the hands of our Intelligence
Bureau in Switzerland, and thus we became
aware that Von Hutier was commanding on this
particular part of our front. It was not difficult
for us to draw the conclusion that he was there
for a purpose.

Our Air Service, from reports and photographs,
was also showing us the growth in the number
of new hospitals and aerodromes on our front,
as well as roads, railways and bridges.

I began at once pointing out to Haig and
G.H.Q. that the forces at my disposal were quite
inadequate to hold my front against the attack,
signs of which were already apparent. With the
force originally at my disposal I could not even
delay them on the forty-two-mile front along which
the Fifth Army was extended. Three more divisions were therefore sent to the Army, arriving by
the middle of February, bringing the total up to
eleven infantry divisions and the Cavalry Corps.
But this force was still most inadequate, and three
more divisions were eventually sent to me, or
moved within reach—the last, the 50th, arriving
in March, shortly before the battle opened.
These, of course, were not in time to do much
in the way of work on defences, etc., and two
of them were kept in G.H.Q. Reserve up to the
last moment. With these reinforcements the
Fifth Army still remained terribly undermanned,

even taking into consideration the fact that it was to fight a delaying action and not a decisive battle.

By the 21st of March the dispositions of the Fifth Army were as follows :

On the right stood the III Corps, now under General Butler, who had come from G.H.Q. to take Pulteney's place, after having been on Haig's Staff since 1915 : this Corps had the 58th, 18th and 14th Divisions in line. I had moved one cavalry division (the 2nd) behind it, the equivalent of one infantry brigade, which was all I could spare.

On the left of the III Corps was the XVIII Corps under Maxse, energetic and resourceful, with the 36th, 30th and 61st Divisions in line, and the 20th in G.H.Q. Reserve, S.W. of Ham, sixteen miles from the battlefield. Watts with the XIX Corps held the next place with the 24th and 66th Divisions in line, and no reserves at his disposal, though I still had two cavalry divisions—the 1st and 3rd, of the Cavalry Corps—behind him, and the 50th Division was in G.H.Q. Reserve, round Rosières, over twenty-five miles from the battlefield.

On my extreme left stood the VII Corps, now under the able command of Walter Congreve. General Snow had cracked his pelvis some time previously, which made him very lame, and in January he had to give up and go home.

The VII Corps consisted of the 16th, 21st and 9th Divisions in line, with the 39th in reserve round the village of Nurlu.

Besides the immense amount of new trenches and wiring required to put my front into a sound defensible state, practically no dugouts existed for the protection of the machine gunners during a bombardment. Some idea of the neglected condition of this front and the immense amount of work which required attention can be gathered when it is realized that the administrative requirements to ensure proper movement and supply in battle were, sixteen narrow-gauge lines, at least four new sidings and platforms on the broad-gauge lines, the maintenance and strengthening of forty roads and the building of at least two new bridges—a colossal task in truth, a race against time, with the Fifth Army in the unpleasant position of being left at the post with a very bad start.

Four trains per diem, carrying stone and metal for the roads, and four trains per diem of engineering material were wanted to fulfil our requirements.

Immediately on my return from French G.Q.G. I wrote to G.H.Q. as follows :

Secret.

Fifth Army,

S.G. 675/41.

GENERAL HEAD-QUARTERS.   1*st February* 1918.

1. I wish to bring to your notice the general situation on my front.

2. The German Eighteenth Army, under General von Hutier, who was so successful at Riga, has

been interpolated opposite my front, additional crossings have been constructed over the St. Quentin–Cambrai Canal, various new hostile aerodromes have been located, a large number of German divisions are in reserve, and good railway facilities to bring them forward rapidly exist. Further, the general situation renders an attack between the Oise and the Scarpe more probable in the immediate future than elsewhere on the British front. The Germans naturally wish to obtain an early decision, and it is probable that active operations can take place on the Oise–Scarpe front, owing to the condition of the ground, some two months before they can be undertaken with reasonable prospects of success further north. Consequently, I think it a not unreasonable conclusion that, if the Germans attack the British Army shortly, the Fifth Army is likely to be involved.

3. Of my 40-mile front, owing to the difficult country south of the River Oise and the course of that river itself, the southern 12 miles are not likely to be the scene of a serious hostile attack, but of the remaining 28 miles of front either the whole or part may well be the subject of a heavy hostile offensive. Should this occur, if I was fortunate enough to obtain sufficient notice of the enemy's intention, I should be able to place some 10 divisions in line, of whom 9 would be disposed from Moy northwards (*vide* attached diagram). This would work to roughly 5500 yards of front per division. I should then have in reserve 1 cavalry division in the III Corps area and 1 division in the XVIII Corps area, 2 cavalry divisions in the Cavalry Corps area and 1 division in the Allaines area. Provided

tactical trains were forthcoming, some 48 hours would be required to complete these dispositions.

By this time, the infantry of two divisions from G.H.Q. Reserve in other Armies would have arrived, and I should then be able to place two more divisions in line, thus reducing the average front per division north of Moy to 4400 yards. This would be satisfactory but would depend entirely on my receiving the necessary 96 hours' notice.

4. The more recent German attacks (*i.e.* Verdun, February 1916, Riga, and the attack on Italy) have been characterized by a short bombardment up to about 6 hours and the most strenuous efforts to obtain surprise. These efforts I cannot be sure of defeating; consequently in his initial attack the enemy might find me disposed as at present, with the equivalent of 8 divisions in line on a 40-miles front : this would naturally go far towards ensuring him success, especially in view of the state of my defences.

5. Strenuous efforts have been made by all to improve the defences : south of the River Omignon, the old French front, they are better than further north ; in a month's time it would be possible to fight a defensive battle between the Oise and the Omignon. Further north the defences are in a backward state, and I cannot expect them to be even satisfactory before the middle of March or in a good state before the end of the month.

6. The very wide area I am responsible for, the condition of the roads, the lack of light railways, the absence of accommodation, the shortage of labour, and the many things (such as Army and Corps R.E. workshops) necessarily lacking in an

area recently organized as an Army Area, have all tended to delay progress.

Then follows a statement of my minimum requirements.

8. Provided that the above can be provided, I consider that by the 15th March the whole of the Battle and Rear Zones could be made into a good defended area.

9. I should then like to put all available labour on to preparing a position east of the Somme, from about Ham, via Bussu to the high ground west of Moislains, with a view to ensuring the retention of the crossings over the Somme.

H. P. Gough,
General,
Commanding Fifth Army.

As fate decreed, we had a long continuance of dry weather, quite exceptional for winter and spring, and by the middle of March the Oise had ceased to be of much value to our defence as a serious obstacle along the twelve miles of its course, nor did sufficient labour arrive in time to enable us thoroughly to complete the Battle Zone, much less the Green Line or Rear Zone, the Péronne bridge-head, and the western bank of the Somme. This letter was written seven weeks before the battle, and on the assumption that there would be enough labour to commence work at once.

Feb. 3. On my return from my visit to French G.Q.G. I called a conference of my Corps Commanders

22

on February 3, and I then outlined my view of our situation as follows :

The main attack might be expected against the Third and Fifth Armies, with Amiens as its objective, for the following reasons :

(*a*) No genuine preparations apparently had been made elsewhere.

(*b*) Von Hutier, who carried out the attack at Riga with the Eighth German Army, had been put in opposite our Fifth Army front in command of the Eighteenth Army. In the Riga attack he relied completely on surprise. All the troops for the attack were kept seventy miles away and only collected in the forward area within five to eight days before the attack. The actual battle was preceded by only six hours' bombardment, no trench mortar or gun emplacements being previously prepared.

(*c*) Good divisions had been withdrawn from the line, which was now held by divisions of poorer quality. The good divisions whilst undergoing training were being reconstituted in their old corps. With all those various indications it was therefore not safe to think no attack was contemplated because things were quiet. The enemy had within an eighty-miles radius of St. Quentin 64 divisions in line and 34 divisions in reserve, beside some 50 further away.

(*d*) It was vitally important to impress on all subordinate commanders that though things were quiet just then, the storm might come at any moment : furthermore, in view of the fact that the Battle of Riga was opened by the enemy forcing the passage of the Dvina, that section of our line guarded by the Oise should not be considered as immune from attack.

In reply to my letter of February 1, G.H.Q. replied firstly by sending a memorandum on " the Principles of Defence on Fifth Army Front," dated February 4, and they followed this up by a letter on the 9th.

In the first they laid down :

Principles of Defence on Fifth Army Front.

1. Of the Fifth Army front the southern 12 miles are unlikely to be the scene of a serious hostile attack owing to the difficulty of the country. Of the remaining 28 miles either the whole or any part may become the scene of a serious hostile offensive. On these 28 miles of front there would normally be 7 divisions in front line, giving the average of nearly 8000 yards per division. This would leave 4 divisions and 3 cavalry divisions in reserve.

. . . . . .

2. In the devastated state of the Fifth Army area communications are one of the primary difficulties for a determined defence of the Battle and Rear Zones.

. . . . . .

We have not the means available to render these communications really efficient south of the line Roisel–Péronne.

. . . . . .

3. To meet the situation as regards communica-

tions, it is for consideration whether our main resistance in the Fifth Army area should not be made behind the line of the River Somme.

.   .   .   .   .   .

It would appear that the whole question is one of communications. In other words, are the communications through Péronne of such importance as to render it advisable to cover that place and fight east of the Somme ? From the transportation point of view these communications are of great importance. The loss of the crossings at Péronne would seriously affect the supply of troops in the centre and northern portions of the Fifth Army area, and this would indirectly affect the maintenance of the positions on the right of the Third Army.

It is considered, therefore, that we should continue at all events to cover Péronne by means of a bridge-head, and that every effort should be made to improve the communications in this vicinity. South of Péronne it will only be possible to improve and develop roads, and it is hoped that this can be done to some extent.

By falling back to the line of the Somme the situation as regards rear communications would be improved, but considerable construction work would still be necessary before it could be considered satisfactory. The German communications would in such a case naturally be very bad.

On the other hand, by falling back to the line of the Somme and Tortille we should have the devastated area of the Somme battlefields immediately in rear of our defensive positions.

5. Although it is considered that we should make

our preparations to fight east of the Somme, we must, however, be prepared to be forced back to the line of the Somme. It is therefore of first importance that an emergency zone should be constructed at once along the line of the Somme and Tortille and connected by a switch to the existing defensive zones north of Péronne, as shown on the attached map. This should include and secure the high ground at Mont St. Quentin.

6. In view of the importance of Péronne it is considered necessary that a bridge-head should be constructed at sufficient distance from that place to cover the crossings there and to protect the railway communications through Brie. This can best be done by the construction of a switch from the present rear zone about Marquaix via Bouvincourt to the emergency zone at about Pargny.

.   .   .   .   .   .

8. The principles on which the defences of the Fifth Army front should be conducted should, it is considered, be similar to those laid down for the other Armies. That is, we should be prepared to fight for the Battle and Rear Zones. It may, however, at any period of the defensive battle become inadvisable to employ large reserves to re-establish either of these zones, in which case a withdrawal to the line Crozat Canal–Somme–Péronne bridge-head—or even to the line Crozat Canal–Somme–Tortille—should be carried out. The possibility of having to execute a withdrawal should receive the careful consideration of the Fifth Army, and detailed plans should be worked out. Each division should be covered by a small rear-guard of all arms. By the skilful handling of these rear-guards,

26

particularly as regards the employment of machine guns in conjunction with wire obstacles, it should be possible to delay considerably the enemy's advance, cause him to expend considerable force and generally dislocate his arrangements.

J. H. DAVIDSON,
M.G.

4th February 1918.

From this memorandum the policy of the Fifth Army was definitely laid down. In spite of the advantages of a retreat to the Somme prior to the battle, we were to prepare to fight east of the Somme, though we must also contemplate being forced back to the line of that river, and to meet this contingency the construction of a bridge-head to cover Péronne was ordered.

This bridge-head was to be some twenty-five miles in length, and another line on the western bank of that river and the Tortille was to be undertaken : this also was about twenty-five miles long, making a total of fifty miles of fortifications. When it is remembered that the Hindenburg Line was about seventy miles and the Germans took some six months to construct it, under what might comparatively be called peace conditions and with a vast army of civilian labour, it was not possible for these defences to be in a forward state in the time at our disposal.

In the letter of February 9 my instructions were amplified :

Fifth Army.   Secret.
O.A.D. 761.

In reply to your S.G. 675/41 dated 1st instant.

1. The Field-Marshal Commanding-in-Chief considers that in the event of a serious attack being made on your Army on a wide front, your policy should be to secure and protect at all costs the important centre of Péronne and the River Somme to the south of that place, while strong counter-attacks should be made both from the direction of Péronne and from the south, possibly assisted by the French Third Army.

2. While the Forward and Battle Zones in the Fifth Army area should be fought generally in accordance with the principles laid down in G.H.Q. No. O.A.D. 291/29, dated 14th December 1917, the provisions of paragraph 6 regarding the reinforcement of the Battle Zone and its re-establishment by counter-attack require some modification. Neither is the ground which these zones immediately protect so important, nor are the communications leading to them so good as to warrant reinforcements being thrown into the fight, counter-attacks on a large scale being launched, or the battle being fought out in the Battle Zone, unless the general situation at the time makes such a course advisable. It may well be desirable to fall back to the rearward defences of Péronne and the Somme while linking up with the Third Army on the north, and preparing for counter-attack.

3. As regards the organization and preparation of the rearward defences, the main considerations in their relative order of importance will be as follows :

(*a*) The protection of the river crossing at Péronne will be secured by a bridge-head. The defences of this bridge-head must be sited with a view to securing our road and rail communications through Brie and Péronne.

The organization and preparations for the defence of the Péronne bridge-head will be completed in detail as soon as possible, including the provision of adequate communications, *i.e.* roads and light railways, also additional bridges over the Somme.

(*b*) The retention of the line of the River Somme will be secured by the construction of an emergency defensive zone as a strong retrenchment along the left bank of that river as far north as Péronne and thence northwards by the Tortille River. In connexion with this defensive zone small bridge-heads will be constructed as required to secure the immediate crossings over the river.

The organization of this emergency defensive zone and the construction of the defences will be carried out, concurrently with the work on the Péronne bridge-head, with such labour as may be available after the requirements of the latter have been fully provided for.

. . . . . .

H. A. Lawrence,
Lt.-General,
Chief of the General Staff.

G.H.Q.
9th February 1918.

Copy to Third Army.

These instructions contemplated the construction of still more lines and switches. Meanwhile our front line and Battle Zone had been neglected, and as already stated they were quite incomplete, with very few if any shell-proof dugouts in them for machine-gun detachments, brigade or battalion head-quarters, dressing stations, etc. These shelters in themselves were always laborious constructions, requiring much time and skilled engineers and miners to complete them.

This letter from G.H.Q. envisaged also the importance of strong counter-attacks, " from the direction of Péronne and from the south, possibly assisted by the French Third Army "—aimed at the flanks of the possible German attack. Such counter-attacks were in accordance with sound tactical principles, but it was quite unpractical to suggest that the Fifth Army, constituted and situated as it was, could carry them out. By the time that the Fifth Army could be established on the Péronne bridge-head, assuming that it ever had the time to complete this, the Army could be in no position, with the troops at its disposal and after the casualties it must by then have suffered, to do more than hold this extensive line. The counter-attack from Péronne could only be made by the British Third Army. It was to that Army that G.H.Q. should have directed this part of these instructions, and supervised carefully the necessary plans for carrying it out.

The troops at the disposal of the Third Army

and the early reinforcements it received justified the hope that it could hold up a German attack on its front and yet spare sufficient troops for such a counter-stroke. But as things turned out, its front line went the first day, and instead of counter-attacking against the right flank of Von der Marwitz's Army, it was driven back from the line of Péronne to behind Albert—a distance of ten miles in thirty-six hours (March 25–26), thus adding to the difficulties of the Fifth Army on its right, and supporting neither the defence of Péronne nor the line of the Somme.

On the 16th of February Sir Douglas Haig Feb. 16. held a conference at Doullens and gave us his appreciation of the situation, which, briefly, came to this : he thought it was unlikely that the enemy would attack on a greater front than thirty or forty miles, as the number of his guns would limit him to such a front.

The attack, however, need not be continuous and could be expected anywhere along the whole front from the Oise to Lens. He thought the destruction of the French coal mines near Bethune might tempt the Germans to attack in that part of our line. He was expecting a prolonged struggle, and this made it advisable to economize his reserves and not use up his divisions too fast.

Brig.-General E. W. Cox, the new Chief of the Intelligence Section at G.H.Q., estimated that the Germans had 178 divisions in France, of which 110 were in line and 68 in reserve. Of those in line, 50 were on the British front.

They could bring over 23 more divisions by May, but it was not likely they would wait as long as that, and he expected an attack in or before March.

Haig then went on to say that he thought the main effort would be against the French, and that the indications from the British front showed no signs of an imminent attack. G.H.Q., influenced by its Intelligence Staff, undoubtedly expected the main German attack to fall on the Third and First Armies, and only its extreme left wing might possibly engage the Fifth Army.

It is not easy to understand how the Commander-in-Chief arrived at some of these conclusions. G.H.Q. Intelligence should have known that the Germans could dispose of plenty of artillery and ammunition, and that they were by no means limited by their artillery to a front of " thirty or forty miles," and all the indications collected on the Fifth Army front pointed clearly to that front as being the one which was most threatened.

There were no signs of a German attack on Bethune, and the French coal-fields did not provide an object of so decisive a character as to ensure victory and peace to the Germans before the American Armies could arrive, and this was almost certainly their aim.

The reports sent in by Lt.-Colonel S. S. Butler,

32

the G.S.O. 1, Intelligence, Fifth Army, together with my letters to G.H.Q., should surely have provided, even by this date, sufficient proof of the imminence of an attack on the British front, and also of its locality ; in the first fortnight of February alone, the Fifth Army, beside noting the presence of General von Hutier in command of an army opposite it, reported to G.H.Q. the presence on its front of 5 new German hospitals, 3 new aerodromes, the arrival of an air squadron from the Flanders front behind St. Quentin, five days on which new work and extensions of German light railways had been observed, a new bridge which had been built over the canal north of St. Quentin, a new ammunition dump, and a marked increase of movement on railways and on roads. The statements of prisoners also were already pointing to the fact that an attack on the front held by the Fifth Army was contemplated. As the weeks went on these became more definite, until we knew almost for certain, more than a week prior to the attack, that March 21 was " *Der Tag.*"

All the various indications continued to grow apace from now on to the day of the attack, all tending to point increasingly to the Fifth Army front being one of the threatened sectors.

During these days Haig came to visit me on several occasions. Before the battle broke out he came with me to have a look at our rear-defences, and on another occasion I took him down to my right flank south of the Oise, where he came up very close to our front in the wooded country near Barisis. During these visits I had an opportunity of discussing with him the situation, and of pointing out to him the great deficiency of men and the backwardness of our defences, and he explained to me his view of the situation. He now fully realized the imminence of a great attack and that it would entail a prolonged and fierce struggle, but though the indications pointed to the attack falling on my front, he still thought it was possible that the German Command was attempting to deceive him, and intended to attack unexpectedly elsewhere, evidence of which can be found in his dispatch where it is stated that he thought the main attack would fall north of the Bapaume–Cambrai road.

On the British front a defeat in the north was a far graver menace than one in the south. Comparatively close behind the left wing in the north lay the ports of Dunkirk, Calais and Boulogne—from twenty to forty miles away. The loss of these ports would have been absolutely fatal to the British Army, and therefore almost certainly decisive of the War.

They must be held at all costs. Haig rightly considered that it was here that he must retain his strength and his reserves until he could see the issue clearly. On the other hand, behind his right a German advance was not by any means so dangerous a threat. The enemy could advance a long way before any vitally serious danger could arise ; here we had, in fact, some room to manœuvre.

Haig was, therefore, absolutely sound in his judgment to keep his reserves in the north, and to leave the Fifth Army to do the best it could with its few divisions to hold up and perhaps exhaust the German forces. I understood this conception perfectly, and in my discussions with Haig it was clearly understood by both of us that the rôle I was to play was to retire gradually, and to delay and exhaust the enemy, without exposing my Army to annihilation. It was, of course, a delicate manœuvre and would require great ability, as well as courage, sacrifice and endurance from officers and men of the Army, but it could be done, and, as events turned out, it was done, thanks to the really astounding endurance and courage of the troops.

A point which Haig, however, had to consider was the just balance between supplying his manœuvring wing, the Fifth Army, with enough divisions for its task, without giving it one too many, or on the other hand leaving it so weak that it could not even carry out its rôle of delaying and exhausting the enemy. It may be said that he achieved this result, but nevertheless he " ran it a bit fine." It was only the great, the gallant, the steadfast self-sacrifice of the battalions, brigades and divisions which made the result possible and brought this manœuvre so completely to a successful conclusion.

The defences of the Péronne bridge-head were, of course, non-existent, and we were to start on them as soon as G.H.Q. could send us any labour.

If our defences had been better, and if we had had the necessary time to repair the neglect of the previous nine months or so, then our task would have been easier. Time was our greatest need. Every day our problem became more clearly apparent. Every day the time for preparation grew less. We were fighting for Time. But the Germans were fighting *against* Time.

II

During February I made the acquaintance of the first combatant contingent of the U.S.A. Army, and also of General Smuts. I had previously had some of the American non-combatant services under me in " teams " of doctors and nurses who had worked in our casualty clearing hospitals during the Passchendaele operations. I now came in contact for the first time with some of the combatant troops of the American Army. This contingent was composed of the 6th, 12th and 14th Regiments of Engineers, and they were at first engaged on the construction of bridges which were urgently needed on the Fifth Army front. I went over one morning to their billets and inspected them —a fine body of tall, strong, active men—and afterwards I had a talk with their officers, not only about their own work, but on our general situation as well. Their experiences during the time they were with us were as exciting as they were varied, and gave them a vivid insight into war and battle. Their first job was to build a bridge over the Somme, but even as they were completing it they had to prepare it for demolition, and eventually when we fell back to the line of the river they blew up their own bridges.

They were then called upon to fight and formed part of that organization afterwards known as " Carey's Force," when they acted as infantry soldiers holding the trenches in front of Villers-Bretonneux against the German attacks, and when parts of the trenches were lost, counter-attacking to regain them and to re-establish the line. Altogether they did very valuable service with the Fifth Army and established most friendly relations with their British colleagues.

I believe that these regiments of engineers were the first of the American Army to fight in the line, and pitched into their first battle as they were, under strenuous and difficult conditions, with things round them looking none too rosy, they showed themselves brave men and stout soldiers ; of course, the desperate battle against odds took a toll of them, as it did of the rest of us.

General Smuts's visit was occasioned by a somewhat furtive desire on the part of the Cabinet to have an independent opinion as to the steps being taken to meet the coming storm, and also to inquire into the responsibility for the disastrous losses in the Battle of Cambrai during the previous November.

He came over, in fact, in the invidious capacity of an unauthorized and irregular inspecting officer on the Army Commanders in France. In spite of these unpromising auspices, I was very pleased to meet Smuts, and enjoyed the few days he spent with me. We got on very well, and were quite open and frank to each other. I showed him and told him everything, and took him round as much of our front as time would permit. He realized easily enough the amount of work which had to be done and the state of previous neglect on our new front, but he was pleased at the great progress we were making to rectify these things. I took him one cold and foggy morning as far forward as Epéhy, which already was well advanced in its defences, with elaborate lines of heavy wire, and this strong point impressed him a good deal. It was these defences, together with the determined and stout hearts of its garrison of the 21st Division, which held up the German attack for twenty-four critical hours during the battle.

In our feverish preparations to meet the German menace, our difficulties were not all directly attributable to our enemies on the other side of No-Man's-Land. The origin of some was to be found at home. Of these, the supply of men to

38

fill our depleted battalions was one of the most serious. The losses involved in over three years of war, fought all over the globe, usually under the pressure of the call to assist an Ally, had undoubtedly been a great drain. Nevertheless hundreds of thousands of men were still retained under arms in England—kept there partly from a ridiculous fear of a German invasion, and partly because the Cabinet actually did not desire to trust Haig with any more men, blaming him for all that 1917 had cost the British. This seems both a weak and an unjust attitude for Mr. Lloyd George and his colleagues to have taken up. The battles of 1917 had been fought with the knowledge and consent of the Cabinet and at the particular demand of the French. Mr. Lloyd George had made a determined effort to place the British Army directly under the orders and control of General Nivelle and of the French General Staff for the Battle of Arras—and indeed for the duration of the War. If the latter part of his plans had been carried out, the British Army would have fought even harder than it did, with correspondingly heavier losses. Our voluntarily-assumed burden was expensive enough. It would have been infinitely more so if we had been merely the humble agents and servants of the French, as was the demand of many persons having little knowledge of the real facts or giving them insufficient thought.

The situation in the early months of 1918, however, was that the Germans were now threatening to attack us in overwhelming force, and every consideration should have been put aside except the vitally important one of ensuring the strength of the British Army to resist that attack successfully. If it had been thought necessary, definite and clear orders could have been given to the Commander-in-Chief as to how his troops should be employed, and that no offensive operations were to be contemplated, but the Army should not have been deliberately kept below establishment at this critical juncture.

In consequence the infantry in France had to be reorganized. Every brigade was reduced from four battalions to three—a loss in itself of one quarter of our strength ; this was intensely serious, but the new grouping induced a further weakness, since it was a new and an untried organization for battle, and one greatly inferior to the original. All our divisions in turn had to undergo this reorganization, which took place early in 1918, and left us considerably weaker from every point of view.

Moreover, the drafts which we were now getting were composed largely of returned wounded. I remember going to Nesle to inspect one such draft. It was not a day I shall easily forget, as it was snowing heavily and nothing would keep the snow out of the inside of the car ; in spite of all windows being shut, by the time I reached Nesle there were three inches of snow on the bottom of the car, and our legs and knees were covered as well. When I walked down the line of this draft I found about half of the men wearing the wound stripe and many wearing two or more. It struck me at the time as unjust to send back such men, who had already faced death and danger, had already suffered more or less severely, while there remained at home many thousands of comparatively young men who had never seen a shot fired. One's heart went out in sympathy and in admiration to those men standing in the square at Nesle that day.

Anxious as was the situation which the Fifth Army faced at this time, my thoughts were not entirely confined to our immediate horizon. The general situation in England provided some cause for anxiety as well. I felt we were nearing a crisis in our fate. I knew that the War would not be decided entirely on the battlefield. This War, to a far greater extent than we had ever before experienced, was being fought by the people themselves. The War could be, perhaps would be, won or lost at home. Russia had already given us an example of this, for her collapse was due first to the disintegration, failure in resolution, and the outbreak of revolution among her people. It was from home that weakness spread to her Army. The same phenomenon was to be seen in Germany before many months were over, but in January 1918 this was still hidden in the lap of the gods, though even at that time I could sense the danger of a possible collapse in Britain herself.

The Army at the front was still as staunch as ever. But at home signs were not wanting that the strain was beginning to tell—articles in the Press, attacking the leaders of the Army and Navy—statements by people in authority—stories brought back to the front from many a London drawing-room. It was reported to me that a civilian who was touring the front got on a wagon in the streets of Péronne, and from this extemporized platform addressed all and sundry who were in the streets of that ruined town. He told the soldiers there that " everyone at home was fed up to the back teeth "—that " if only the soldiers would refuse to fight there would be peace " ! This last sentence expressed a fallacy which is often the outcome of a combination of ill-regulated thought and badly-digested sentiment. If the soldiers of the Fifth Army had refused to fight (and this gentleman in company with all his fellow-countrymen may thank God that they did not !), the only peace which we could have obtained would have been one dictated by the Germans after a disastrous and disgraceful defeat.

Though such terribly irresponsible appeals fortunately fell on deaf ears, they were a sign of the state of mind of some people in the country, and it behoved all of us who were in any way responsible for leadership to take note of it.

Sir Aylmer Hunter-Weston was not only a Corps Commander, but also a Member of Parliament, and as I knew he was at home at that time, I wrote to him and begged him make a speech in the House of Commons which would do something to cheer and hearten our people, to show them that the state of Germany was worse than our own, and to appeal for steadfastness, courage and resolution, those great qualities of our race, so necessary at this moment. Hunter-Weston did make a speech to this effect, which, coming from him, a serving soldier, had a very great effect. It was much quoted in the Press, in speeches all over the country, and copies were made for distribution in factories, schools and clubs all over the country.

In this letter I pointed out that though Germany was in sore straits, her people starving and longing for peace, yet her leaders well knew how often brave and resolute people, even in the most desperate straits, have won because they were superior in that one quality—Resolution.

We were in much the same position—it had come to a contest in Resolution between the British and the German peoples. To encourage Britain, to keep her steadfast, we must realize that behind this great barrier of German trenches, barbed wire, and brave soldiers—which, like a dam, held back our advance—a work of steady disintegration was going on. No one could see what was happening at the base of that dam, but suddenly it would burst and the flood pour through.

I said that I did not think the German people could stand the pressure another year, and it behoved us to remain hopeful, resolute and courageous. The situation was really better than it looked.

As far as my own Army was concerned, I felt it my duty to tell officers and men frankly of the menace looming beyond our trenches, but at the same time to appeal to their virtues, their courage, their sense of duty, and the great traditions behind them. I issued a call to the officers and men, but realizing that in so great a machine as a modern army I could not speak to every one, I asked my Divisional Commanders to help me.

I recalled the objects for which we had entered the War, and quoted the words of Abraham Lincoln in a crisis of the American Civil War, when he said :

" We accepted this war for one object, a worthy object, and the war will end when that object is attained. Under God, I hope it will never end until that time."

And finally, I said :

" I would call to your memory—you, the soldiers of to-day—the great deeds that have been performed in the past by the regiments to which you belong, deeds which speak to us from the pages of History, from the old church walls of England, deeds in foreign lands against

44

many different foes, but always the same cause
—the freedom of our Country."

III

The Fifth Army, accused of many sins of
omission in the first moments of panic which
had swept over London and through the country,
had in reality laboured strenuously to prepare
itself to meet the coming storm and to make
good in the time available the deficiencies existing
on its unprepared front.   In spite of all difficulties,
the worn and tired troops, forced· to adopt a
new organization, loyally gave up all ideas of
rest and training, and dug, wired, and carried
stores and ammunition with whole-hearted energy.

Many of the steps taken by the Army were new.
The following are some examples.   In January
we informed G.H.Q. that all the bridges in our
area should be prepared for demolition, which
was agreed.   Lists of all the bridges in each corps
area were drawn up and the corps engineers instructed to inspect them and place the necessary
charges, fuses, etc., in position in weatherproof
covers.   In every case a special party was defin-
·itely detailed to blow up the bridge in case of
necessity, and all concerned knew their mission.
The only exceptions were the railway bridges
belonging to the French.   They and our own
railway service objected to their destruction being carried out by the Army, and they undertook to blow them up themselves should necessity

arise ; G.H.Q. assented to this suggestion, and in consequence we were forbidden to touch them. On March 10 the Fifth Army wrote to G.H.Q. that its engineers were

> in close touch with the O.C. the French Railway Troops operating the Chemin de Fer du Nord. All that requires to be done is to ensure that the commander of these railway troops should receive orders from his superiors to act in accordance with the attached instructions.
>
> I should be glad if you could arrange for this to be done, and if the matter could be treated as urgent.

It does not seem that G.H.Q. took up this matter sufficiently seriously, for when the time came the French failed to blow them up, but the Fifth Army during its retreat destroyed over 250 bridges for which it was responsible.

By March 21 we had had two months of dry weather, and the Somme, never a large river above Péronne, was very low—about four feet of water in most places. In a few cases our charges did not act as effectively as they were expected to, and here and there a girder or two still stood and allowed the German infantry to scramble across, and in all cases the wreckage falling into the comparatively shallow water created islands and steps which helped the Germans to cross. But these were conditions over which we had no control.

Certain important road and railway bridges

behind the German lines and within range of our guns were selected, and orders issued for their systematic destruction by a concentrated bombardment, once we were certain of the imminence of the German attack. They were not to be fired on before that, however, lest such action should arouse suspicion and give the Germans time to establish alternative routes. This bombardment of German bridges actually began on March 14 and was effectively carried out.

Orders to " prepare for battle " and " man battle positions " were drawn up and issued, and the procedure was periodically practised. The result of these orders was that when the attack did break over the Fifth Army, every man of the few available was " on parade," as a private once described it to me. I may say that he added that " we need not bother about those who criticized the Fifth Army but who were not on parade on the 21st of March." Certain localities of tactical importance on every brigade front were reconnoitred, and the companies which were in reserve for counter-attack purposes were specially instructed to be ready to retake these and were, during their tour of that duty, regularly practised over the ground. Several counter-attacks made by troops in the battle had actually been practised previously exactly as they were eventually carried out.

Tanks were still too new an arm to have a code of tactical instructions for all occasions, and so far we had had no experience of their use in defence. It was in the Fifth Army that their employment in this capacity was first worked out. The Tanks were placed in sections of two or three attached to the counter-attack troops, and were moved into position concealed from the air close to these troops. There they were retained till the battle opened, and their action along the front in close co-operation with the supports was most useful and enabled many points to hold up and delay the German attackers for hours. The rest of the Tanks with the Army were kept further back under the orders of the various Corps Commanders.

But we also had to anticipate the possibility of the employment of Tanks by the enemy, and this question also was very thoroughly considered. I admit I was genuinely very anxious on this subject. There is no doubt that the effect of efficient Tanks would have been enormous on our front in exploiting an already overwhelming attack. The Germans had had plenty of time to create a force of Tanks, for, from examination of those they had captured from us in previous years, they would have been saved the trouble of experiments with the mechanism.

The steps we took to meet this possible danger were, first, to move forward single field guns, carefully hidden, within 2000 yards of the front line. These guns were never to open fire till the enemy's infantry advanced, so as to ensure their presence remaining a secret. About eight of these guns per corps were placed in these forward positions—a total of over thirty. But besides this, after a thorough reconnaissance of the ground, Tank mines were laid in certain localities over which it was thought any advancing Tanks must pass. These mined areas had to be carefully marked to prevent our own troops crossing them and blowing themselves up.

We also turned our attention to the use of aeroplanes in defence, and in conjunction with General Charlton (who was now commanding the Air Force in the Fifth Army) we drew up a plan for specially designated aeroplanes to engage the attacking infantry and the known batteries by flying low and using their machine guns. Weeks before the attack the pilots for this duty were detailed and knew their task and the ground over which they were to operate.

Before February, we issued instructions to the four Corps Commanders that all the personnel of the various schools—such as the Artillery Schools, the Infantry Schools, the Trench Mortar Schools, the Sniping Schools—were to be looked on as immediate reinforcements in case of necessity, and that their employment was to be thought out and provided for in all schemes of defence.

In addition to the usual lines of trenches, wire, etc., the Fifth Army had arranged for a line of redoubts for all-round defence to be prepared and garrisoned. These were sited on localities

49

of tactical importance, from 1000 to 2000 yards behind the front line, and there was one on almost every battalion front. These redoubts performed most effective service, and in almost all cases were most gallantly defended.

Certain of our most forward hospitals, Casualty Clearing Stations being their official title, were evacuated before the battle and brought back considerably to the rear.

Finally, the morale side was not neglected, and besides the appeal which I made to the whole of the Fifth Army through my Divisional Commanders, I was at times asked to speak to the troops and on all these occasions I stuck to one theme, which can be deduced from a copy of some notes in pencil which I found among my papers—and which I give here as originally written :

What our Country now demands from her soldiers.
The Germans will attack—their weight, their hopes.
It is their last card.
If that fails—all is lost, for them.
It will fail—if we stand firm.
But this is a crisis.
What we fight for—necessary to nerve ourselves.
We entered war with Enthusiasm—
But now—must be carried on—with Patience, Perseverance, Dogged Courage.
But these qualities required at home also.
We soldiers must realize that it is the People at war.
We must help those at home by our own cheerfulness—our own courage.

50

So far, spoken to you as Citizens—

Now a few words as soldiers—

Remember our Traditions.

We are now responsible for a great Trust.

When the time comes—let us be—Ready.

Vigilant.

Resolute.

Cheerful.

When we have secured—Our Homes—our Honour —and Peace.

Then our children can say that we failed not in our duty, we handed them a great and noble Heritage.

These may sound exaggerated words in these days, sixteen years after the War, when it is not so much the fashion to set duty and sacrifice for others in the forefront of our conduct in life, but in those distant days such words, spoken to officers and men who understood something of the reality of these matters and of the magnitude of the task before them, did not fall, I believe, on deaf ears. The Fifth Army did respond to the call of Duty ; it did fight the German effort to a standstill ; it did shatter their last hope ; it was ready, vigilant, resolute and cheerful, under conditions of danger, terror, fatigue to a degree to which no other soldiers have ever been exposed. They " stuck it out " grimly.

Moreover, I verily believe that the appeal to our great race is always most potent when it is made to its courage, to its sense of duty ; when it calls for self-sacrifice, for noble aims, rather than to self-interest, or hatred, or to the baser passions. I have such a faith in my countrymen wherever they are found all over the world that I am sure they will always do their duty if they are told what it is, and are asked to do it. That is still the great cry to the heart of our people ; nor do I think that such appeals, on the rare occasions when they are required, should be dismissed as purely hot air.

When all the defensive measures of the Fifth Army are studied, and when the thorough way in which they were gone into is seen (as is evident in the official instructions, letters, etc.), it can hardly be said that with the time and forces available much was neglected which the wit of man could devise for making good our defence.

Over some vital matters we had no control : the number of men at our disposal ; the long-continued dry weather in mid-winter prior to March 21 ; and then dense fog.

As to the numbers at our disposal, Brig.-General E. A. Wood wrote to me on April 23, 1925, and said : " Our last meeting was on 19th March 1918—when I was holding the front line at Fort Vandreuil, with my brigade—the 55th (18th Division). You came up with the Corps Commander, General Butler, and I remember your severe criticisms on the thinness of my line over a vast front."

My own activities during these weeks of preparation were naturally confined a good deal to

52

the office, studying reports and maps, discussing and drawing up with the Army Staff the issue of orders and instructions, corresponding with G.H.Q. and my neighbours. But I got out often enough to go along all our forty-two miles of front, and see nearly all the Divisional and Brigade Commanders at one time or another. I used to make rough notes of what I saw and ask the corps concerned about the matters on my return.

As a sample which may prove of interest, here are some of my notes made one morning during a tour of the fronts of the VII and Cavalry Corps.

1. Security of troops in rear—not attended to. Picquets wanted in proportion to strength of force, not merely sentries—example—St. Emilie, Ronssoy. Templeux Quarries. Frequent inspection by Div. Staffs necessary.

2. Garrisons of Posts—not clear as to duties—or best use of fire—no idea of mutual support, or value enfilade fire—all fire direct. Again—frequent inspection by Staffs wanted.

3. Plans of defence—too disjointed.
Too much left to juniors.
But plans belong to seniors.
Result—badly laid out defences—no mutual support—only isolated and direct defence.

4. 1 battalion—at Villers-Faucon—support to brigade 4000 yards from Epéhy—over an hour's march. What are its orders? Is it to reinforce and hold Epéhy? If so—what posts is it to occupy?

5. 2 battalions—Reserve Brigade. Longavesnes.
   4000 from rear—Battle Zone—1 hour. What
   are their orders?

   Should move to Saulcourt (2 miles) on order—
   " prepare for battle "—

6. Ronssoy—and Lempire (two villages which ran
   into one)—held by one battalion, very small
   for so large a place.

   If Reserve Battalions are to go up to Ronssoy,
   how do they fit in with present garrison?

   What posts do they occupy? Do they know
   them?

7. 24th Division.

   Reserve Brigade—Montigny—Bernes 2 to 3
   hours' march.

   Cannot some battalions be kept forward—at
   Hesbécourt—Hervilly—?

   Anyhow—to move there—on " prepare for
   battle " order—

   3rd Cav. Div.—one brigade—one battalion at
   Vadencourt—

   What is its rôle—its orders—?

   Who is responsible for defence Le Verguier?

8. Discipline at Schools.

   Comfort of officers and men.

These notes give some idea of the life of an
Army Commander in the field, and his duties.
Constant inspection and instruction by the higher
Staffs were needed. Many points which were
noted would have been dealt with by Battalion
and Brigade Commanders in the days of a pro-
fessional and fully-trained army, but though the

constant fighting of the previous year had taught officers much and nerved them for the fray, it had left them ignorant of much which they should have known but which they never had the time to learn.

The system of Army Schools for junior officers was designed to meet this difficulty. A certain proportion of the officers and N.C.O.s were withdrawn in turn from the line and sent to these schools for a couple of months, in order to get an all-round training, which they could not acquire in the trenches. But the system fulfilled another essential object ; it gave our greatly strained young officers and N.C.O.s a complete change and some comfort, brought them back to civilization and to a certain amount of good cheer. I used to go down, when possible, at the end of each course to give away the prizes, and sometimes dined at the school mess afterwards. It reminded me of the " *bonne camaraderie* " of old days in the Army—toasts, songs and a bear-fight.

It was on one of these occasions that I found a contingent of young American officers who had just finished the course with our own. They were a delightful lot of young men, frank, cheerful, desperately keen to learn, modest and free from all jealousy. They presented the school with a gramophone as an expression of gratitude for the good time they had passed there. The presentation was accompanied by speeches, toasts, etc., in which chaff, fun and wit were conspicuous. In the subsequent bear-fight, which I surveyed from the safe vantage point of the doorway, it was impossible to differentiate between British and Americans ; the hurly-burly of merry shouting youngsters was a kaleidoscope of happy augury.

One wondered how men could so quickly throw aside the memories of the desperate enterprise they were engaged on, how quickly they could change to earnest, stern, resolute leaders in battle. But human nature is largely made that way, at least the best of it is ; it is well that it is so, otherwise we could never carry on in times of great suffering, and should lose half the happiness of life. The capacity for recovery from mental and physical shock and strain is one of the highest tests of character and vitality. It was an attribute desperately needed and doggedly applied by all ranks of the Fifth Army in the weeks that were to come.

IV [1]

Der Tag was now approaching. We were nearly certain of the day.

Very early on March 19, the last pieces of evidence from the Fifth Army front regarding the approaching storm were gathered. A German artillery non-commissioned officer captured west of Bony, an aeroplane pilot brought down near Ly.-

[1] See Sketch Map 2, facing p. 70.

Fontaine, infantry prisoners captured south-west of Villers-Guislain, and Alsatian deserters from a trench-mortar battery south of St. Quentin, all told the same story, each in his own way—in some cases, it is true, unwittingly. The sources of information were not only independent, but the prisoners were of widely differing types : and the news they gave, corroborating many other indications, completed the last link in the chain of evidence gradually forged during the preceding weeks. All these matters were reported by " urgent operations priority " telegrams to G.H.Q., and after several long telephone conversations between the writer [1] and Cox it was agreed that the final details as regards the date and hour of the enemy's attack, the nature of the preliminary gas bombardment, the German reserves available, etc., were now in our possession.[1]

On 19th March I wrote to my wife :

I expect a bombardment will begin to-morrow night, last six or eight hours, and then will come the German infantry on Thursday, 21st.

. . . . . .

Everyone is calm and very confident. All is ready.

The final steps over which the Fifth Army had control were now taken.

On March 18 I had moved the 2nd Cavalry

[1] Lt.-Colonel F. S. G. Piggott, in an article in *The Army Quarterly*, January 1925. Lt.-Colonel Piggott, in March 1918, was G.S.O. 1 (Intelligence), Fifth Army.

Division (General Greenly) down to the right as a reserve to Butler's III Corps. It was the only reserve at the disposal of this Corps, which was holding a front of eighteen miles. I also moved the 39th Division a little closer to Congreve's front, VII Corps.

The 20th Division was fifteen miles behind the front of the XVIII Corps, and I wanted to move it up five to eight miles further northward, to Ham and north of it. In addition, I wished to move forward the 50th Division at least a day's march and bring it across to the east side of the Somme—as it was more than twenty-five miles behind our front—and I asked authority of G.H.Q. for these moves. These steps were in my opinion most urgent, almost vital. G.H.Q. refused to allow me to move a man.

The Chief of the Staff spoke to me on the telephone one evening after dinner, about the 19th, and said that it was not sound to move reserves before the situation was clear, that to move them up would be to tie them down, and that " they would be committed." He thought it a mistake to have moved the 2nd Cavalry Division to the III Corps. These moves, he said, were premature. He spoke in general terms, and gave me, in fact, a little lecture on the conduct of military operations in accordance with the teachings of the great Masters. I was quite well aware of these principles, but they did not apply to the situation in which the Fifth

Army was placed at that moment. We knew we were to be attacked in overwhelming force. We knew our line was dangerously thin, and that the fighting which the difficult and delicate rôle of a delaying action and the "*manœuvre en retraite*" imposed on us must involve a prolonged struggle, and it was important to spare the troops as much hustle and fatigue as possible. Moreover, all the lessons of the War, both in attack and defence, had taught us how important it was, once your action was decided on, to close up the supports and reserves behind the line. No one had suffered more from the failure to recognize this principle than had Haig himself at the Battle of Loos, when Sir John French had denied him the use of his reserves till too late.

The admonitions of the Chief of the Staff therefore failed to impress me. I could not understand his point of view under the circumstances, and I answered that to move up reserves close behind the threatened points was an equally well-known axiom, and I thought these two divisions should certainly be moved forward.

I failed, however, to obtain the sanction of G.H.Q., and I never discovered if Lawrence was delivering me a message from Haig or representing the General Staff view of the case.

In any case, I thought it was a grave mistake at the time, and events and further consideration have not made me change my opinion. I knew a great deal more of the circumstances on my front and grasped the situation facing us a great deal more clearly than did G.H.Q. at this time —or, in fact, at any time during this battle.

It is impossible for me to say that G.H.Q. showed a full understanding of the circumstances and progress of the battle. Neither the Chief of the Staff nor any senior Staff Officer visited me personally during its course. I believe some junior officers from G.H.Q. were sent to visit the divisions and may have come into the Army office and talked to the junior members of the Army Staff, but I never saw them. I believe they reported that, in spite of the desperate odds and the heavy losses of the strenuous retreat, the spirit of officers and men was splendid and their courage unabated. I dare say they found the same atmosphere existing at Army Head-quarters—for it certainly did. But these casual visits of junior officers were far from being the steps which the situation demanded. By 10 a.m. on March 21 G.H.Q. must have known the magnitude of the attack. Officers of their senior Staff might have been with me, in the early afternoon at latest, and perhaps daily during the ensuing days of the fighting. I could have made the situation much clearer to them personally than was possible on the telephone. They might have helped considerably in the co-ordination of the action of the two Armies.

During the whole eight days' battle, the only

member of G.H.Q. who came to see and hear things for himself was Haig. He came and saw me once—on Saturday, the 23rd. We did not go at all into details of the situation, nor of the action of the Third Army. The possibilities of its holding up the German advances on my flank, and the chance of success of a heavy counter-attack by this Army on my left and the great effect such action would have had, were not discussed. Haig was calm and cheerful, but all he said to me was: "Well, Hubert, one can't

ERRATA

P. 60.—The statement that the Chief of the Staff, Sir Herbert Lawrence, did not visit me during the progress of the battle, is not correct. He came to see me on the afternoon of Sunday, March 24.

I much regret the error.

P. 141. *Lines 5 and 6.*—" Monday the 25th " should be " Tuesday the 26th."

them. If the attack had not come and they had not been required, they could easily have been withdrawn and dispatched elsewhere. To move them up was not to commit them. I still consider that retaining them under G.H.Q. so long was an error, and that they should have been placed under my orders on arrival in my area. Though

61

Haig could not, quite justifiably when the strategical situation is considered, send the Fifth Army any further material support, G.H.Q. might have helped in other directions more than they did. In several matters the Fifth Army was not too well served. G.H.Q. had refused to give me the Chief of the Staff for whom I asked ; they removed General Pulteney from the III Corps and sent General Butler shortly before the battle without consulting me ; they took away the commander of the 50th Division, General Clifford Coffin, V.C., without giving me any warning or asking my opinion, on the eve of battle itself, and appointed in his place a Brigadier who was in one of the Divisions engaged on the III Corps front (General H. C. Jackson) ; he could not be immediately spared to take over his new command, and, in any case, was a complete stranger to it. This left the 50th Division to be commanded in the greatest battle we had yet fought by the next senior officer, to chance in fact, and he was not the man for such a task. Furthermore, Lt.-Colonel S. S. Butler, the head of my Intelligence Section, was taken to G.H.Q. *on the* 18*th of March*, and Lt.-Colonel P. R. C. Commings, A.Q.M.G.—the second senior on the Administrative, or Q side, under Hambro—was moved to G.H.Q. on March 17.

The two cavalry divisions of the Indian Army, moreover, were also withdrawn from the Fifth Army at this critical moment, and sent to Palestine. At the moment the battle opened they were embarking at Marseilles and were of no use to anyone. For this reduction in my strength I do not think G.H.Q. was responsible. This was due to the Chief of the Imperial General Staff in England and the Cabinet, but perhaps a strong protest and a more convincing assertion of the imminence of the storm might have retained these two divisions for a few weeks longer at the spot where the great decision was being fought out. They would have been a valuable reinforcement.

On Sunday, 17th—St. Patrick's Day—the 20th Division had some sports and an Officers' Jumping Competition, for which I entered both my chargers. In the afternoon I went down to have a chat with the officers of this division and rode my two horses, one of them being fourth out of a total of 120 entries. I did this not only for the sake of a ride round the jumping course, which I enjoyed, but because I thought it was good to meet the 20th Division and see its members under friendly conditions, and also to show some calm confidence in the outcome of the great events before us. I remembered that the Duke of Wellington attended the Duchess of Richmond's Ball in Brussels just before Waterloo, and that one of his principal reasons for doing so was the same. I felt I had a good precedent for thus spending my Sunday afternoon.

During March the Germans began bombing

us severely at night, wherever a target was to
be found. About a week before the battle they
attacked Congreve's Head-quarters, which were
established in a group of huts, with little or no
bomb-proof protection. A Member of Parliament had come out to visit my Army, and I
sent him for a night or two to stay with Congreve
and study our front there. He was unlucky
enough to be there during this attack, and it
must have brought home to him in full force
the horrors and terrors of war. A succession of
German planes dropped bombs on these Head-
quarters for several hours. Congreve and his
Staff had just sat down to dinner, but in spite
of the terrific explosions all round, Congreve
sat quietly on and ate his dinner entirely un-
moved. All the wind-screens and every pane of
glass of the motors attached to Corps Head-
quarters were smashed, but otherwise not a car
was touched. Two officers and three men were
killed—the wonder was that they were not all
blown to bits.

A night or two afterwards, the Germans
dropped some bombs on Nesle, close to my
Head-quarters. I went out to see what mischief
had been done, and found a bomb had dropped
on a shed used as a billet by a company of one
of our Labour battalions ; several men were
lying among the wreckage, dead or wounded.
I bent over one man in the dark, an old labourer
of about fifty years of age. He was quite calm,

though this must have been his first experience of war at close quarters, and in spite of the great shock that the explosion of a bomb causes, he said to me, " I am going ; put your hand into my jacket and pull out my pocket-book and write what I tell you." I said, " Oh no, you just keep quiet and rest yourself." But he insisted, and said, " I want to have everything settled up nicely for my missus." It struck me as a wonderful tribute to his coolness, his courage, his thought for others. I flattered myself that perhaps it was only among the British such a spirit could have existed under similar conditions.

On Tuesday, the 19th, it began to rain, and this continued at intervals during the next day—the first rain for nearly eight weeks. This was the prime cause of the very heavy fog and mist which so handicapped our unfortunate troops during the first three days or so of the battle. I went round all my four Corps Commanders on Wednesday to have a final talk over everything before the battle. With Army Head-quarters some thirty miles behind the front, a journey of this kind took up a large part of the day.

At this stage—on the very eve of the battle, so to speak—it is convenient and pertinent to give some details of the German forces opposed to the Fifth and Third Armies.

On our extreme right, south of the Oise, General Boehn's Seventh Army had 2 divisions facing 2 brigades of our 58th Division—but made no attack.

From La Fère, for five miles northwards, was Gayl's Corps of 4 divisions, facing 1 brigade of our 58th, and 1 brigade of our 18th Division.

From here to the north, as far as the Omignon River, stood Von Hutier's Eighteenth Army with 13 divisions in front line and 8 in second line, a total of 21 divisions.

To meet him stood 4 divisions, and two brigades of the 18th Division, of our III and XVIII Corps, with the equivalent of another brigade, in the form of the 2nd Cavalry Division, in support. It might be fair perhaps also to count the 20th Division in G.H.Q. Reserve, though it was fifteen miles from the front, and could not get into the fight on March 21.

North of Von Hutier's Army was the German Second Army under Von der Marwitz. It stretched northwards from the Omignon River, as far as our left, and beyond it had 4 divisions still further north, facing 3 divisions of Byng's Third Army in the Flesquières salient, but these made no attack on the 21st.

Von der Marwitz's Army attacked the Fifth Army with 13 divisions in front line, and 4 in second line, a total of 17 divisions. To resist this attack stood 5 British divisions of our XIX and VII Corps in front line, with 1 division (the 39th) in support, and the equivalent of 1 brigade in the form of the 1st Cavalry Division.

66

North of Von der Marwitz's Army was the Seventeenth Army under Von Bülow. He delivered a secondary attack on the Third Army, north of the Flesquières salient, with 9 divisions in front line and 6 in second line, a total of 15 divisions. To oppose this attack the Third Army was able to employ 8 divisions on March 21.

The odds in the actual attack against the two British Armies on March 21 were, therefore :

	1 Brigade 58th Division 1 Brigade 18th Division	opposing	Boehn's Seventh Army	Gayl's Corps of 4 divisions
FIFTH ARMY	III and XVIII Corps, with equivalent of 5 divisions	,,	Von Hutier's Eighteenth Army	21 divisions
	XIX and VII Corps, with $6\frac{1}{3}$ divisions	,,	Von der Marwitz's Second Army	17 divisions
THIRD ARMY	8 divisions	,,	Von Bülow's Seventeenth Army	15 divisions

A total of 42 German divisions against 12 British in the Fifth Army
and 15 German divisions against 8 British in the Third Army
or a grand total of 57 German divisions against 20 British

Behind Von Hutier there were 8 more divisions coming up, 4 of which were within 8 miles of the front on March 21, while to the rear of Von der Marwitz were a further 4 divisions.

The Fifth Army had behind it—
The 20th and 50th Divisions, which got into action on the 22nd.

One French division (125th), which came
    into action on the 23rd.

The 8th British Division, which began to
    arrive on the 23rd.

Two more French divisions, which arrived
    on the battlefield by the 24th (9th and 1st
    Dismounted Cavalry Division).

Total reinforcements up to 24th March—6
    divisions.

The enormous odds facing the Fifth Army
are thus immediately apparent. Furthermore, it
should be remembered that while the German
divisions had been strongly reinforced, our own
were grievously under establishment—the average
strength of our battalions scarcely exceeding 600
men. This, coupled with the loss of a battalion
per brigade, to which I have previously referred,
meant that each division was reduced practically
to one-half of its former infantry strength.

Some critics have asked the reason why the
Germans were able to hold our attack in the Ypres
series of battles in 1917, whilst we on our part
were forced to give so much ground in 1918.
An elementary consideration of the facts would
provide the answer. On July 31, 1917, we
attacked with eight divisions, supported by one
division of the Second Army on our right, and
two French divisions on our left. After a lapse
of weeks further attacks were carried out. This
system had been generally adopted by both the

French and the Germans, as well as ourselves, in all previous attacks on the Western Front. It enabled the attacking troops to be relieved and spared, but it could not hope for rapid and decisive results. The system evolved and put into force by the Germans in this battle was quite different. The attack was made on four times the front, with more than four times the number of divisions all massed against the part to be attacked and all close up, so that nearly all could move forward almost simultaneously. This ensured an overwhelming force and the maintenance of the battle in full and vigorous activity for days and nights without intermission, which gave the defence no rest, allowed little or no time to bring up fresh divisions, and made the systematic relief of tired ones most difficult.

Then the great extent of front which the Fifth Army was called on to hold only allowed one man per yard of its widely-flung line. The situation would at once have been altered immensely in its favour without making any other change in the figures involved in the problem if the front could have been reduced from forty-two miles to, say, twenty-one.

The actual odds (in men) against my Army on the opening of the battle were four to one. It is interesting to note that in no previous assault during the whole of the War had the ratio of attackers to defenders exceeded two to one.

Though as early as the 3rd of February, during my conference with my Corps Commanders, I had outlined the possibility of an attack by fifty or more German divisions, it remained an uncertainty until the actual day whether this mass would be thrown against the whole of the Fifth Army front, or only against part of it.

At that time, of course, I was unaware of the full magnitude of the coming attack. I knew that it was to be no light blow which the Fifth Army had to meet, but no calculations of any of the Allied Staffs had allowed for such a concentration against us. The Fifth Army Staff alone had foreseen that such an attack was possible.

.   .   .   .   .   .

The night of March 20 every man in the Fifth Army whose duty allowed him to do so, lay down calmly enough for a night's sleep, but all of us felt perfectly certain that we would be wakened before morning by the roar of battle. And so we were!

II

THE BATTLE OF ST. QUENTIN

II

THE BATTLE OF ST. QUENTIN

The Storm Breaks—News from the Corps—Inaction of
G.H.Q.—The Battle Day by Day—A Fighting Re-
treat Ordered—Filling Gaps—The Retirement behind
the Somme—Difficulties of the Third Army—The
South African Brigade—Extemporized Battalions—
The Visit of Foch—The Last Assaults—Relief of the
Fifth Army—Aftermath—Conclusion.

I [1]

AT 10 minutes past 5 I was awakened by the Thursday, roar of a bombardment, which, though March 21. it sounded dully in my room in Nesle, was so sustained and steady that it at once gave me the impression of some crushing, smashing power. I jumped out of bed and walked across the passage to the telephone in my office and called up the General Staff. On what part of our front was the bombardment falling? The answer came back almost immediately : " All four corps report heavy bombardment along their front. Third Army report bombardment on about ten miles of the southern part of their front. The French

[1] See Sketch Map 3, facing p. 104.

report no bombardment on their front. No signs of any infantry advance as yet." This at once opened my eyes to the magnitude of the attack on the Fifth Army. It dispelled with brutality any lingering hopes and ideas that I might further thin out some unthreatened part of my line and concentrate more troops against the main German attack, and perhaps collect enough to launch a powerful counter-attack. Obviously, that was not to be ; the problem was more simple, though far more terrible and menacing. The whole thin line was involved, and our few supports, reserves, and all the energies of our minds and bodies would be called on to maintain it intact along its whole length.

We issued a few orders, and warned all concerned. Troops in reserve, under G.H.Q. or not, were ordered to be ready to move. At the moment there was nothing more to be done. All the necessary steps to meet the storm had been taken : the German infantry would not attack for several hours. I looked out of my window, and in the morning light I could see that there was a thick fog, such as we had not yet experienced during the whole of the winter. We were getting into spring, and it was extraordinary to have so dense a fog at this date. Very dimly I could see the branches of a tree in the garden about forty feet from my window. The stars in their courses seemed to be fighting for the Germans. But it was imperative that we should

74

not be discouraged ; it was necessary to make a further call on our hearts for Resolution, determining that we would win, cost what it might, in the end, even if all went against us at first.

I threw myself back on my bed, and went to sleep for an hour. By 8.30, shaved, bathed and fed, I was back at the telephone, but no reports of the German advance had yet reached us. I was convinced of the magnitude of the attack by now, the bombardment continuing unabated and reports having come in of the smashing effect on our trenches and wire. Our batteries were being smothered by gas shells, but in spite of all the personnel having to wear their masks—a great handicap to violent exertion—they were firing rapidly on known targets " by the map "—for nothing could be seen owing to the fog, and they could not therefore fire on anything visible. Our aeroplanes could not get into the air, nor could the pilots have seen anything if they had succeeded in doing so : our plans for their employment, therefore, were of no avail, or, at any rate, could not be put into force till hours had passed and the fog had begun to lift.

This was no moment for delay or awaiting authority. I therefore sent orders to the two divisions in G.H.Q. Reserve : to the 20th to march on Ham, and come under the XVIII Corps orders as soon as possible ; to the 50th Division to get ready immediately to entrain the

75

infantry and send the artillery by road, to come under the orders of the XIX Corps.

Having warned and started these two divisions, I called up G.H.Q. and asked for their authority to move them, which was now granted. I found myself speaking to General Davidson. I asked when we could expect support, and I told him that we certainly should want it. He told me that all the G.H.Q. arrangements for moving down fresh divisions to our front were being set in action : but these arrangements were to send four divisions to the Third Army first, and that the fifth division would be sent to me ; " I could not expect it for 72 hours." That would be Sunday morning. The question came into my mind, could we last as long ? It was asking a good deal of the Fifth Army. As events turned out, this division actually arrived a little sooner.

During the morning reports of the action began to come in, and we knew something of what was taking place along our front. The terrific bombardment had cut most of our signal wires and prevented our runners from getting back with messages, most of them becoming casualties long before they could reach their destination, while the fog prevented all observation or visual signalling. The reports therefore were still meagre and scrappy, and did not enable either Corps or Army Head-quarters to be absolutely sure of the true course of events. Meanwhile, though the fog was now lifting, the din and roar of battle

76

continued. Roads, especially cross-roads, aerodromes and our back areas were being kept under a heavy fire by long-range guns.

The German gunners had not only an enormous concentration of guns and trench mortars, but also plenty of ammunition, and they were firing at a tremendous rate, so much so that it was said that in many instances their guns became so hot that periodical pauses were necessary to cool them. It was on this preponderance of artillery that the Germans depended for the first phase of the assault in the blasting of a gap through which the masses of infantry could pass. Their hopes were high and their anticipations extensive : based on their experiences at the Battles of Riga and Caporetto, the two German Armies of Hutier and Marwitz expected to reach the line of the Crozat Canal and the Somme as far north as Péronne by the evening of the 21st of March.

But when the first fateful day of the struggle closed they were far from attaining these objectives, thanks to the gallantry, the sense of duty, the heroic self-sacrifice of the officers and men of the Fifth Army.

In the Forward Zone of our defence, thinly held by about twenty battalions on the whole front of nearly forty miles, eight or nine battalions entirely sacrificed themselves and disappeared, but not before they had inflicted very heavy losses on the Germans, and had already begun to wear out many of the enemy divisions. If there had been no fog the German losses would in all probability have been doubled.

The battlefield consisted of bare open plateaux, with long spurs after the nature of fingers, running east and west.

Between these fingers lay broad deep valleys. Of woods there were few, and those more of the nature of copses, with the exception of Holnon Wood, strongly prepared for defence, in the centre of the XVIII Corps line.

Although our trenches were continuous, our line was not so by any means. Our numbers were far too few to permit of our maintaining a continuous line. Our front, therefore, was held by isolated posts, in irregular and zigzag lines, so laid out that the posts, and machine guns in particular, could fire along long belts of wire and take an attacking enemy in enfilade. The posts were drawn back in the valleys, with the object of firing across and sweeping the opposite spurs. Our forward guns were also placed at the end of valleys to sweep not only the valley but also the spurs on either side. To obtain the full power of such a defensive system a visibility of 1000 yards at least was required.

But the fog on the 21st reduced the visibility to 20 yards, and our elaborate arrangements of flank defences were brought to naught. The garrisons of the isolated posts could do nothing but wait till they could see their foes, which was not possible until the latter were within 20 to 50 yards, by which time the first wave of the attack had often already passed behind them. There was then nothing left to the posts but to fight it out as best they could, each a little island among a sea of enemies, alone and unsupported. Moreover, the bombardment had caused heavy casualties, many of our posts being annihilated by the artillery fire before a single German appeared, and many others losing a large proportion of their effectives.

Before 10.30 a.m. reports came in :

The III Corps—the 18th Division had repulsed an attack, and the 14th Division said it was fighting in the forward and battle positions.

The XVIII Corps reported its line intact.

The XIX Corps—the 66th Division reported that the situation seemed developing.

The VII Corps reported attacks on Quentin Ridge and Gauche Wood—held by the 9th Division.

Soon after this, the III Corps reported that the enemy, debouching from La Fère, had taken the Forward Zone held by a brigade of the 58th Division.

Between 10.30 and 11.30 a.m. reports reached us at Army Head-quarters that the attack was general along the whole Army front, and that everywhere the enemy had penetrated our Forward Zone, though many isolated redoubts were gallantly holding out and were still able to communicate with their divisions and corps.

79

At 12.15 p.m. the XIX Corps reported that their "Front Battle Zone was being turned from the north." This pointed to the capture of Ronssoy, and this was confirmed shortly afterwards by the 16th Division who had been holding that village. Congreve—VII Corps—reported that he was dealing with this situation, and sending up some reserves. He said the 21st and 9th Divisions were holding their line firmly, although heavy fighting was going on.

Such were the first messages which came in to our Head-quarters.

About 1 p.m. the fog had lifted sufficiently for our aeroplanes to get into the air, and shortly afterwards we heard from them that masses of Germans could be seen moving forward, and that the roads in their rear for ten to fifteen miles were "packed with troops."

It was evident that the Germans were attacking in overwhelming masses along almost the whole length of the Fifth Army front.

The III Corps reported the loss of the important villages of Essigny and Benay in its Battle Zone, and that the 14th Division had suffered very heavy losses. I talked to Butler on the telephone. He had only the 2nd Cavalry Division in reserve, the equivalent of one infantry brigade, and his line was 18,000 yards long. He did not think it possible then, or later on, to launch so small a force in order to retake these villages, and I agreed. It would have required at least a division,

80

and that ready and on the spot, to have successfully counter-attacked against them.

It was now evident that the German attack was so serious that I could not hope to fight it out successfully in the Battle Zone, but must carry out a delaying action, which would aim at saving the Army from complete annihilation, but which would enable it at the same time to maintain an intact, though battered and thin, line in face of the German masses until such time as the British and French Commands could send up sufficient troops to hold the ground.

In adopting this policy we would fight hard enough to inflict very heavy losses on the Germans, wear them down and perhaps exhaust them. Our Supreme Command would then be in a position to strike a powerful, possibly a decisive and final blow.

This reasoning was reinforced by the instructions I had already received from Haig, confirmed in writing by the letter of February 9 from G.H.Q. already quoted. Moreover, I knew by now how small were the resources on which I could rely in order to play the delicate rôle allotted to the Fifth Army.

From the British Army I could expect one division [1] in three days, and one more the following day. From French sources, one division

[1] As already stated, the first division to arrive (the 8th) began to appear in line in two days, but I did not at the time expect it before the third day.

would be with me ready to take its place in the battlefield after two days, and then I might hope for two more after three days ; a total of five fresh divisions in action by the fifth day of battle, a help certainly, but—when a front of over forty miles had to be reinforced—still quite insufficient to bring to a standstill the German masses which would also be receiving reinforcement. We must look forward to maintaining the struggle for at least eight days. Our losses in the Forward Zone, where our battalions had so faithfully and steadfastly fought it out, and had been almost annihilated in doing so, had proved what the result of a decisive battle would be.

The French Sixth Army in position on our right informed me it was sending one division across the Oise on Friday, but it would not be in line till Saturday morning, the 23rd, and General Humbert, who was commanding the Third French Army, in reserve behind our right, informed me that no troops had been placed at his disposal by General Pétain for co-operation with me.

The particular rôle of Humbert's Army, as I had been given to understand, was to move up to our support in case of necessity, and to take over again its original front, relieving the Fifth Army.

The majority of its divisions, however, had been moved to other parts of the French front, in view of possible German attacks, as already stated.

In a narrative by the German Staff [1] on this battle it appears that when discussing the attack on the British Army, Sauberzweig, Chief of the Staff, Second Army, said, " The French will not hurry themselves to the help of their Ally when attacked. They will wait first to see if they will not themselves be attacked on their front, and they will not decide to assist their Ally until the situation is completely cleared up for them. This will be late, for demonstrations will be executed by the Crown Prince's Group of Armies to deceive the French."

It seems that the German Staff had arrived at a fairly accurate conclusion as to how events would influence the minds and the action of the French.

Later on, Humbert came in to see me, and when I said something to the effect that it was a desperate struggle and that I was glad to see him with his Army, he replied, " *Mais, je n'ai que mon fanion,*" referring to the little pennant on his motor with the Army colours. This, however, was not exactly the aid that we were looking for at that moment !

I spoke on the telephone to all the four Corps Commanders during the early afternoon, and told them that our policy was to fight a delaying action, holding up the enemy as long as possible, without involving the troops in a decisive struggle to hold any one position.

[1] *The Army Quarterly*, January, 1929.

This was confirmed next morning by the following telegraphic order :

> 10.45 a.m.—In the event of serious hostile attack Corps will fight rear-guard action back to forward line of Rear Zone and if necessary to rear line of Rear Zone. Most important that Corps should keep close touch with each other and carry out retirement in close touch with each other and Corps belonging to armies on flank.

Immediately after my telephone conversation with the Corps Commanders, I got into a car and went round to see them. Owing to the rapid movement of events, I could not be away too long from the telephone, so I was only able to pay each a hurried visit. Before I started—about 3 o'clock—I ordered the 3rd Cavalry Division to move down at once to the support of the III Corps, and it reached its destination by 10 that evening.

III Corps. Butler was the first of the Corps Commanders whom I visited, as the situation seemed more serious here than elsewhere, and it was necessary to decide what steps should be taken on this flank before deciding on the course of action of the other Corps. I found him perhaps a little anxious, but this, of course, was very natural in view of the situation. The fact of losing ground and guns in his first battle as a commander pressed rather heavily upon him, and it was not, of course, an encouraging start-off. However, I did not let

84

him worry much about that ; the Corps had had to encounter enormous odds, and now the only thing which mattered was to take the right steps to meet the menacing storm.

His left—14th Division—had been very severely handled, and driven back a considerable distance, thus exposing the left of the 18th Division, the right of which was also being threatened from La Fère.   We decided, therefore, to draw back his whole Corps behind the Crozat Canal, and I told him that I was reinforcing him with the 3rd Cavalry Division.

I found Maxse and his Staff cheerful, active and confident, and thus they remained through- out the whole of the battle. His XVIII Corps had done magnificently, and after desperate fight- ing still held its Battle Zone intact. The nine battalions, however, holding its Forward Zone had sacrificed themselves, bravely and stoutly, and had been almost annihilated in doing so.

In spite of the firm front which the XVIII Corps could still show, both its flanks were seriously threatened, its right by the loss of Essigny on the III Corps front, and its left by the loss of Maissemy by the XIX Corps.   Maxse and I arranged, therefore, that he should continue to hold his Battle Zone as long as possible on Friday, the 22nd, but that he should draw back his right flank, to keep touch with the III Corps which was withdrawing to the line of the Crozat Canal, and that he should also throw back his left to cover

XVIII Corps.

the Omignon Valley and keep touch with the XIX Corps.

Though Watts's XIX Corps had not lost as much ground as the III Corps, it was facing perhaps the most serious prospect on the front of the Fifth Army ; for the odds against it were heavy, its troops were few, and any reserves on which it could count were a long way behind it. It consisted of only two weak divisions, the 24th and the 66th, with the 1st Cavalry Division in support. The 50th Division, which I had allocated to Watts, was too far away to be any use that day, and he was only able to get it hurriedly into position by Friday morning, after it had spent a day in the train and had marched all night.

The Forward Zone of this Corps had also been overrun, and its right driven back considerably. It had lost Maissemy in the Battle Zone early in the day, but in its centre the 8th Queen's in Le Verguier were maintaining a stout defence. On the left, which the loss of Ronssoy by the 16th Division of the VII Corps had exposed, the line had also been driven back to the village of Templeux.

Watts was a spare, active man, quiet and very modest in demeanour, but one of the most courageous and experienced of our commanders. Having retired from the Army previous to the War, he returned on its outbreak and was at once put in command of one of the brigades of

86

the 7th Division, intended for the relief of Antwerp. Since then, engaged in almost every battle, he had risen to the command of a corps. His judgment, sane as it was courageous, was an inestimable asset to his Corps, and to me.

My instructions to Watts were to hold his present front as long as possible, but to bend back his left and there keep in touch with the VII Corps.

Congreve's Corps had maintained its Battle Zone intact on the left where it was in touch with the Third Army (V Corps), but its right had been pressed back considerably and Ronssoy lost. Acting with decision and energy, Congreve had brought up the 39th Division and built up a new front with one of its brigades. The 21st Division was still holding Epéhy in spite of the desperate assaults of the Germans, and the 9th Division had also brought the German attack to a standstill in front of its Battle Zone. VII Corps.

The fall of Ronssoy left the 2nd Royal Irish Regiment almost isolated in the neighbouring village of Lempire. Here, almost completely surrounded, it held on with great tenacity till 2 p.m. against overwhelming assaults, and long after that hour some posts were still bravely holding out.

The Munsters holding the hill south of Epéhy fought on until 5 p.m., and then the remnants fell back into the village and played a gallant part in its defence until it eventually fell next day.

About 5 p.m. the news of the conditions on the Third Army front came in and made its position clear to us. The Germans had attacked its front north of the Flesquières salient, and had driven in a wedge to a depth of three miles or so, and were already across the Bapaume-Cambrai high road in front of, or in actual possession of, the villages of Demicourt, Doignies, and Beaumetz. This was indeed a very serious threat to Byng's V Corps, which had three of its five divisions in the Flesquières salient. Their retreat was now compromised. He had decided, therefore, to withdraw this corps to his Battle Zone, which was behind the left of my 9th Division—which was still holding the Forward Zone. The retirement of the Third Army would leave my left in the air, and Congreve therefore was obliged to withdraw this division during the night.

Except for the few miles south of the Oise, the fighting along our whole front had been close and desperate throughout the day, many counter-attacks had been made on the enemy, some of which were successful and threw him back for a time. The officers and men of the Fifth Army along almost our whole front had been exposed to a terribly hard and exhausting day ; the Corps and Divisional Commanders, called upon to meet constantly changing situations in the ebb and flow of the violent battle, had to guard new flanks, fill sudden breaches, keep in touch with their neighbours, to find troops for these various

88

tasks as best they could with their very small resources, and to decide with rapidity and act with decision.

Some of the redoubts in the Forward Zone were still holding out. The officer commanding the 7th West Kents had got a message through saying : " Holding out—Boche all round within fifty yards—can only see fifty yards, so it is difficult to kill the blighters."

The defence of Manchester Hill in the Forward Zone is another instance of the heroic behaviour of our troops. This hill—opposite St. Quentin, on the front of the 30th Division—was held by the 16th Manchester Regiment, under Lt.-Colonel Elstob. On taking over the defence of this position, he had already impressed on his battalion that " there is only one degree of resistance and that is to the last round, and to the last man." This injunction was heroically carried out to the letter. At about 11 a.m. Colonel Elstob reported to his brigade that the Germans were swarming round his redoubt. At about 2 p.m. he said that most of his men were killed or wounded, that he himself was wounded, that they were all nearly dead-beat, that the Germans had got into the redoubt, and hand-to-hand fighting was going on. He was still quite cheery. At 3.30 p.m. he answered a call on the telephone and said that very few were left and the end was nearly come. After that, communication ceased. Wounded three times, using his revolver,

G

throwing bombs himself, and firing a rifle, he was last seen on the fire-step, and when called on to surrender by Germans within thirty yards, replied "Never!" upon which he was shot dead.

Before the battered position fell, the Germans had brought up field guns to within sixty yards of the redoubt. For "this most gallant and heroic conduct" (to quote the words of the *Gazette*) Elstob was posthumously awarded the V.C.

To such a leader and to the men who followed him, England owes a debt of gratitude and a measure of admiration which it is impossible to express adequately.

There are countless similar stories of the heroic spirit and the astounding gallantry and energy of officers and men engaged in these days of battle, but the reader must seek them in private letters, regimental histories, the *Official History*, and in Mr. Shaw Sparrow's book.

The 21st of March, terribly strenuous day as it had been, was only the beginning of the great struggle which faced the officers and men of the Fifth Army. They were to endure a continuous strain for eight days and more, and as the casualties grew and the brigades and divisions became daily smaller, even greater calls were to be made on their energy, their courage, their endurance.

In no direction can evidence of this energy be seen more clearly than in the capacity for improvising fighting formations of all and sundry, of creating makeshift companies, battalions and even brigades, which so many displayed. Hunt's Force, Carey's Force, Harman's Detachment, were examples of this energetic improvisation, as will be mentioned later.

The result of the first day's battle could be considered satisfactory and as a magnificent effort. We had identified over forty German divisions actively engaged against the Fifth Army. Their losses had been very heavy but the odds were still enormously in their favour, and many fresh divisions were, we knew, marching up close behind the front of attack. On our side the Fifth Army had hardly any fresh men with which to strengthen its line or relieve any of the battered divisions. The line had been thin on the morning of March 21, but the heavy casualties of the day necessarily caused it to be a great deal thinner on the morning of March 22. Those who still stood in the line had been through a terrific day. How did they keep it up for eight days? I never cease to wonder. It was, I think, their invincible courage, sense of duty, profound belief that Britain, in the end, is never beaten, and perhaps also that strong sense of humour which can see at times the ridiculous in the most terrible situations.

That evening after dinner I had a talk to the Chief of the General Staff on the telephone, and told him of our day and the situation in front of us. I said the Army had done splendidly in holding against such enormous odds practically the whole of its Battle Zone with the exception of the three breaches in our line, at Essigny, Maissemy and Ronssoy. I told him of the number of divisions which the Germans had brought into action against us, and the masses still in rear. I then went on to express very considerable anxiety for the next and following days. The Germans would certainly continue to push their attack on the next day, Friday, and it would undoubtedly continue with unabated fury for many days. Could our tired and attenuated line maintain the struggle without support? That was the question, and it was a grave one. Lawrence did not seem to grasp the seriousness of the situation; he thought that "the Germans would not come on again the next day"; "after the severe losses they had suffered," he thought that they "would be busy clearing the battlefield," "collecting their wounded, reorganizing and resting their tired troops."

I disagreed emphatically, but I failed to make much impression. It has always been my opinion that G.H.Q. did not fully grasp the magnitude of the assault on the Fifth Army or the desperate odds which it had to contend with, and this may have accounted for the misconceptions that were allowed to circulate so freely, even in the Cabinet, during the following weeks.

It has been said that G.H.Q. were misled by my optimism. I do not know that I gave them any valid reason for reaching such a conclusion ; certainly my official letters can hardly be said to justify it. I may have hoped to hold the line against some forms of attack and may have said so, but in this case almost the whole available force of the German attack was thrown against the Fifth Army, and when I recognized the unpleasant fact and the necessity for the policy of a battle in retreat which it entailed, G.H.Q. seemed slow to grasp the implications. I found it difficult to get the full gravity of the situation understood. The impression I gained from Lawrence was that he was trying to encourage me and to cheer me up, but that was not what I was wanting. I was quite ready to deal with facts, however menacing, and to handle the situation, however precarious it might be, but it was important that G.H.Q. should realize the position, stripped of all illusions, and I began to think that I had not succeeded in making G.H.Q. understand.

The telephone should not be the only means of communication, and though of immense service it is not sufficient when grave situations have to be examined in all their bearings. Then personal contact is of vital importance. The failure of G.H.Q. Staff to maintain this personal contact, and thus to ensure the necessary co-ordination between the Third and Fifth Armies, was perhaps one of the weakest features of the direction of the battle.

II [1]

Friday,
March 22.

When day broke on Friday the Fifth Army had taken up its new alignments, and though the eleven divisions which had been engaged holding its forty miles of front had suffered heavy casualties, the corps and divisions had managed to get a few fresh troops into line. The III Corps had withdrawn successfully behind the Crozat Canal and had reinforced its new front with some cavalry, from the 2nd Cavalry Division.

III
Corps.

The fog was as thick as ever in the early morning, and in the III Corps area, the Germans, not knowing the exact positions of our men, did not advance in force till about 11 a.m., when the fog had begun to clear a little. After many hours of fierce fighting they succeeded at 7.30 p.m. in capturing Tergnier from the 8th Londons (58th Division). But some posts still held out and were fighting in the village next morning ; in fact one post fought on and held its position till 5 p.m. that evening (Saturday).

North of Tergnier the Germans succeeded in forcing the passage of the Canal, and thus the right of the III Corps was pushed back. Along the rest of the front the Germans attacked the Corps posted behind the Canal fiercely all day and at times gained a footing on our side of the Canal, but resolute counter-attacks drove them back once more, and when the day was over

[1] See Sketch Map 3, facing p. 104.

our men were still holding most of their positions along the Canal.

The French were now sending this Corps some help. Their Sixth Army on our immediate right moved the 125th Division across the Oise, and this division reached a position in reserve about Chauny during the afternoon (22nd) and its artillery came into action.

Meanwhile the 58th Division on our extreme right had come under the orders of the French. This was in accordance with the agreement previously made between our G.H.Q. and French G.Q.G., that in case of attack the French would take over once more their original front and thus relieve the British troops. On the XVIII Corps front fighting began earlier than on that of the III Corps and went on much later—till after midnight, in fact. Up to the early afternoon a fierce struggle was carried on along the front of the position held in the morning. Many German attacks were repulsed, and on several occasions when they succeeded in gaining a footing in our line gallant counter-attacks made by the few available troops in reserve often succeeded in temporarily recapturing the lost ground. But the battalions were suffering heavy casualties, and Maxse felt that they could not hold on against the continuous and persistent attacks of Von Hutier's Army without being eventually overwhelmed. He had also received the Army order to fight a rear-guard action, and therefore by 1 p.m. he

XVIII Corps.

issued an order to his Corps to retire behind the
Somme. The brigades broke off the fight, therefore, and commenced to retire a distance of eight
or nine miles covered by the 20th Division,
but this was only done at the cost of much
severe fighting.

One brigade of the 20th Division was south
of the Somme; the other two brigades (six
battalions) held a line of over 14,000 yards to
cover the retirement of the 30th and 61st Divisions. It was a very thin line, even for a rear-
guard, amounting to about 1 man to $3\frac{1}{2}$ yards
of front. But these six battalions served their
purpose, and held up the German advance sufficiently to allow the remainder of the Corps to
cross the river. The Germans pressed on with
energy and in great force, and under their
energetic and resolute leadership there were no
signs of " clearing the previous day's battlefield "
or " reorganizing their troops." They meant to
overwhelm us if they could.

Before dawn next morning (Saturday) the
XVIII Corps was established along the Somme
on both sides of Ham, with the 36th Division on
its right—in touch with the III Corps on the
Crozat Canal—the 30th in the centre, and the
20th on the left. The 61st had been pulled back
behind the 20th in reserve, with the prospect
before it of a few hours' rest. The bend of the
Somme forms a bow here and was not parallel
with the original front, rather lengthening the

XVIII Corps line with the left further back than the right. The result of this was that the left of the Corps was now no longer in touch with its left-hand neighbour, the XIX Corps, which was still some three miles east of the Somme, and this caused Watts grave anxiety, which was naturally reflected in my Head-quarters. It upset our plans and demanded new decisions.

Such moments of anxiety were of course of frequent occurrence in this great battle when the long thin line was constantly swaying, opening and closing under the tremendous stress and pressure to which it was exposed from the overwhelming numbers, the energetic leadership, and the efficiency of the German Armies.

It called for a great effort of will to deal decidedly and resolutely with these threats as they arose ; the demand was made of all ranks, from the highest to the lowest, struggling desperately to maintain an unbroken front.

On the XIX Corps front a heavy bombardment XIX of its positions began at 4 a.m. By 7 a.m. the Corps. Germans were vigorously attacking the 66th Division, and before 8.30 they were at the 24th Division. The latter repulsed the first attack with heavy loss to the enemy, but before 10 a.m. Le Verguier, on the front of our Battle Zone, fell. This village was most gallantly and stubbornly defended for nearly twenty-four hours by the 8th Queen's, and before it was finally in the hands of the Germans it had been attacked by five battalions and the artillery of two divisions, from three sides. Colonel Piers eventually withdrew what remained of his battalion, but immediately took up a new position and continued the fight a few hundred yards from the village. Trinket redoubt, also held by men of the 24th Division, repulsed many attacks and was not captured till 1 p.m. During the previous day and night the 50th Division had been coming up by train and road and by 8 a.m. its three brigades were in position from Caulaincourt to Boucly—a front of about 14,000 yards—to cover the retirement of the rest of the XIX Corps. The long and tiring journey inevitably meant that the division was not in the best physical condition to meet the strain which it was to be called upon to face. Moreover, its commander had been taken away just before the battle. Shortly after 12 noon the 24th Division began its retirement, and eventually it was concentrated in rear of the right of the 50th Division.

On the 66th Division front the mist hung thickly in the Cologne Valley, and at first the Germans, pressing vigorously down this valley on the left of this division and the right of the VII Corps, succeeded in gaining a good deal of ground. But small parties of various units manned tactical points in rear and thus checked their advance.

Counter-attacks by supporting troops also fell upon the Germans. The 8th and 19th Hussars with six Tanks drove them back into Hesbécourt, and for a time stayed their advance.

But the 16th Division (VII Corps) on the left was beginning to retire, and therefore the XIX Corps ordered both the 66th and 24th Divisions to retire behind the 50th Division. This was successfully carried out under cover of small forces who fought heroically. In one case forty men of the 15th Hussars and 2nd/6th Lancashire Fusiliers held out till fifteen only were left; eventually these were surrounded and overwhelmed.

The Germans continued pushing on with their usual energy and determination, and by 4.30 p.m. heavy attacks were being made on the 50th Division. After bitter fighting, involving attack and counter-attack, their superior numbers enabled them to take Caulaincourt on the right about 6 p.m. In the centre our line held, inflicting heavy casualties on the Germans, but on the left Nobescourt Farm was lost.

Watts reported the situation to me. He wished to withdraw the 50th Division, and I concurred. Under cover of darkness, therefore, between 11 p.m. and 5 a.m. on Saturday, the 23rd, the 50th withdrew about two miles and took up a new line, Monchy-Lagache–Vraignes–Brusle.

The outlook for the next day on Watts's front was a serious one. The losses among his divisions had again been very heavy. They had all been fighting desperately or marching for two days and one night. Having held on bravely during the day, he now found his right very much in the air at Monchy-Lagache owing to the retirement of the XVIII Corps behind the Somme. He immediately took steps to deal with this threat, and the 24th Division, instead of getting a few hours' rest, was ordered forward once more to cover the right of the Corps. Before dawn on Saturday, the 23rd, it was in position south of Monchy-Lagache as far west as Guizancourt, but this did not completely fill the gap which still existed between the two Corps. Accordingly the 1st Cavalry Division, which by evening had been collected, was also moved south in the early hours of Saturday to the right of the 24th Division, to hold the crossings of the Somme at Béthencourt and Pargny.

The 66th Division also was not allowed a night's rest, but was moved across the Somme and took position to hold the river from Eterpigny to Péronne, a front of three miles.

The 8th Division, my first British reinforcement, was due to arrive on Friday night, detraining from four to sixteen miles west of the Somme. It was placed under Watts's Command, and he directed it to hold the Somme from Pargny to Eterpigny. Only one brigade, however, was able—and that only partially—to get into position by dawn on Saturday, the 23rd.

Watts's XIX Corps front, like that of the XVIII Corps, had now considerably increased— from 13,000 yards to 21,000 yards.

On the left of the Fifth Army the VII Corps had also had a day of very severe fighting. In company with Watts's XIX Corps, the 16th Division was heavily bombarded from 4 till 7 a.m. and then attacked in great force down the Cologne Valley. The Germans, driving back the left of the XIX Corps, turned and enfiladed the right of the 16th Division and forced it back. The rest of the division repulsed all attacks till about 11 a.m. when, orders for a retirement having been given, the units withdrew to the next position, fighting a well-organized rear-guard action. Near St. Emilie, however, three companies of different battalions—1st Munsters, 6th Connaughts, and 13th Royal Sussex—did not get the order to retire. When they found they had been left behind, they fought on rather than surrender, and it was not until 4 p.m. on Friday, the 22nd, when, short of ammunition and greatly reduced, they were finally overpowered.

Meanwhile the 39th Division from reserve had, under Congreve's orders, taken up a covering position. Epéhy and its sister village Peizière were still resisting all attacks, and continued to do so for many hours, till finally, with Epéhy in the hands of the enemy, Peizière was evacuated about noon. On the left of the Corps powerful attacks were made on the 9th Division, and Chapel Hill, gallantly held by the South African Brigade, fell about noon.

After 4 p.m. renewed attacks were hurled at

the Corps' new front, and by dusk it had fallen back to the line Tincourt–behind Liéramont–Nurlu–Equancourt. One company of the 9th Division still hung on to its post at Revelon Farm, surrounded, bombarded by artillery, trench mortars, and even aeroplanes; it was finally overwhelmed about 6 p.m., having, in the words of a German account, " covered the retreat of the main body even to the extent of being destroyed itself."

Another platoon, left in the front of the Battle Zone behind Gouzeaucourt, maintained itself till 10 at night, when its commander marched off in the dark for four miles through the Germans, attacking several parties *en route*, and eventually bringing his men back to the new position. Here the left of the Fifth Army found a considerable gap of two and a half miles, the Third Army's right not having fallen back so far. This gap caused Congreve considerable anxiety, but by the evening the V Corps had pushed forward a brigade (99th, 2nd Division) from reserve; this filled part of the gap, and the rest of it was successfully blocked by the following morning.

During these two first days of battle the artillery of the Army had well served their comrades of the other arms, and in many instances had sacrificed themselves. Terribly hampered by the fog in the early mornings the guns fired " by the map," often until the enemy was on top of them and even round them. They fired at times point-blank, getting their guns away under close machine-gun fire : at other times they had to abandon their guns, as teams could not be got up. Then the officers and men, on their own gallant initiative, formed themselves into small groups, seized perhaps an abandoned machine gun, and fought on as infantry, performing most effective service in a heroic but matter-of-fact way which is beyond praise. Some of our single forward guns fired every round they had—450 each— with terrible effect on the enemy at close range. Two guns fired 1900 rounds before they were knocked out.

The Fifth Army during the first two days had lost about 350 field guns and 150 heavy guns, but largely, thanks to the great activity and energy of General Uniacke commanding the artillery of the Army, these losses were replaced from reserves and gun parks, some of which were under G.H.Q. control. But considerations of routine did not prevent Uniacke from getting things done promptly, and he laid his strong hands on guns in any place where they were to be found, organized the personnel required, and sent them forward again into the line of battle as rapidly as possible.

III [1]

Owing to the forced retirement of divisions, all Head-quarters had to fall back, and Maxse's Staff went back to Nesle, while we had to pack up and

Saturday, March 23.

[1] See Sketch Map 3, facing p. 104.

get back to the next knot of communication wires, which was at my original Head-quarters at Villers-Bretonneux.

Saturday morning therefore found me established there. The situation of the Army continued to be critical. Though the III Corps still hung on to the Crozat Canal, the long line of the Somme, thinly held and running back in a bow considerably to the left rear, placed it in a precarious salient.

Similarly the XVIII Corps, holding this long bend of the Somme with Ham as its centre, and now facing north and north-east, might find its right in a dangerous position if and when the III Corps fell back.

The XIX Corps in the centre, still five or six miles east of the Somme, had its right flank very exposed and its front was very thinly held by weary troops. The VII Corps on its left, also with very attenuated ranks, was still further forward, thus also exposing its right flank, while its left was in an even more precarious position, as the V Corps of the Third Army, though holding ground in front of the VII Corps, had left a wide gap which it had not yet filled.

These positions were not those of my own choosing, but they were forced on me by the varying pressure on the fronts of the different corps. But such as they were we had to deal with them, and they demanded the exercise of decision to rectify and adjust them—some at

III Corps.

XVIII Corps.

XIX Corps.

VII Corps.

once, and others later in the day as the situation developed.

The first thing to do on this morning was to get XIX Corps. the two divisions of the XIX Corps, the 24th and the 50th, back behind the Somme in line with the XVIII, and orders for this were issued before dawn. The line of the river in their rear was held by troops previously withdrawn, viz. the 66th Division on the left near Péronne, and the 1st Cavalry Division on the right. Moreover, the 8th Division, our first British reinforcement, was arriving. Its first brigade got hastily into position on the Somme about 7 a.m., but the next brigade did not take position till 5 p.m.

The morning fog was again lying thickly over the battlefield At times it favoured our men in allowing them to get away unseen. On other occasions it was a source of great danger to our rear-guards, allowing the enemy to approach unseen and surround them. A retirement by daylight is a difficult operation, but it was successfully accomplished, although at the expense of some severe rear-guard fighting in which many companies sacrificed themselves, fighting at times hand-to-hand against greatly superior numbers. By 3 p.m. the 24th and 50th Divisions were safely back across the Somme.

Meanwhile serious events were occurring on III Corps. both the right and the left. On the right of the Army the first French division to arrive, the 125th, had got into position on Friday evening, and one of its regiments (equivalent to our brigade) launched a counter-attack on the early morning, with a view to recapturing Tergnier. But the French were tired after a day and a night of marching, were short of ammunition, which we could not supply, and were hampered by the fog. Their attack failed, though Colonel Bushell of the 7th Queen's, weary as were his men, led them forward again, and taking charge of the French line as well as of his own, carried the attack forward : though severely wounded, he kept the line firm until he fainted.

The Germans early renewed their attacks in great strength all along the Canal front, and before midday they had forced back our hard-pressed troops composed of infantry, cavalry, engineers, and details from many units, as well as the French, to a line about two miles from the Canal. Thus pressure was now developing on the right of the XVIII Corps, facing north along the Somme. To add to the difficulties of the division on this flank (36th), the Germans early in the morning got hold of Ham and crossed the Somme to the east of it. They were enabled to do this on account of the thinness of the line, and the consequent inevitable gaps : the fog also covered them. They drove a wedge into the XVIII Corps front here, southwards; but failed to extend westwards owing to the resolute bearing, the gallant counter-attacks, and the energetic steps taken by all concerned to improvise some

XVIII Corps.

106

fighting force to oppose them. One of these counter-attacks was made by a brigade of the 61st Division, now reduced to a hundred men !

Here the III Corps pushed up a mixed force of cavalry, of 600 infantry, collected from men returning from leave, reinforcements, and men of a Balloon Company, and placed it under General Harman of the 3rd Cavalry Division. This force took up a position to block the centre of the XVIII Corps and protect the rear of the III Corps. When night fell the 36th Division found itself facing at the same time east, north, and west. To extricate it from such a position called for prompt action on the part of the commanders concerned, but the Divisional Commander did not withdraw his line till late the following morning, and to remain thus long demanded much courage and self-sacrifice from some of his units.

The left of the XVIII Corps held the line of the Somme successfully during the day and the following night, much severe fighting going on all the time. Some of the 8th Division had begun to arrive on the Somme, and a few of the French 10th Division had also arrived and taken up a line a little behind the centre of the Corps.

Anxieties were not confined to the right and centre ; the left of the Army, under Congreve, was meeting its full share. Marwitz was throwing the full force of his Army against us, and now, bringing forward his right, he seriously attacked for the first time the V Corps on the extreme

VII Corps.

right of the Third Army, which he roughly handled during this and subsequent days.

Perhaps as a result of this attack the V Corps was unable to keep in touch with the left of the Fifth Army, thereby adding enormously to Congreve's difficulties, and to the strain which his gallant divisions were called upon to support. Moreover, before nightfall the V Corps was driven out of its positions and forced to retire in a north-westerly direction, thus increasing the gap, until by dawn on Sunday, the 24th, one and a half miles of country lay open to an enterprising enemy, in spite of the fact that Congreve had stretched his line until it was covering three miles of ground which lay within the Third Army's boundary. When the Fifth Army Staff informed the latter of this situation, however, it promised to fill the gap.

During the day Congreve's VII Corps was forced back about seven miles on its right and four on its left, fighting desperately all the way till 10 p.m.

It had been a strenuous day for us all ; before 4 a.m. I was talking on the telephone to Congreve and Watts. At midnight messages were still coming in and instructions going out of our office. The fighting had been fierce, and often at close quarters.

Up to 12 (noon) this day, the Intelligence Section of the Army Staff, now under Lt.-Colonel F. S. G. Piggott, had identified forty-five German divisions opposite the Army front, and this number it reported to G.H.Q. as " conservative." The rapidity with which these identifications were made and reported reflected great credit on the Intelligence Staffs of the Corps and divisions, and also on the organization of the Signal Service —for which Colonel E. G. Godfrey-Faussett was responsible.

At 12.20 p.m. on the 23rd, Saturday, G.H.Q. issued an order to the Third Army to prepare a line from the Somme through Albert, to Gommecourt, with a switch line from Bray on the Somme to Albert. Evidently the prospect of the retreat of the Third Army was already being seriously considered.

But at 5.30 p.m. G.H.Q. issued a further order, which said :

> Fifth Army must hold the Somme at all costs. There must be no withdrawal from this line. It is of the greatest importance that the Fifth Army should effect a junction with the French on their right without delay. Third and Fifth Armies must keep in closest touch in order to secure their junction and must mutually assist each other in maintaining Péronne as a pivot.

The line of the Somme, as far as it was an obstacle to an advance from the east, was only a small proportion of the whole extent of the vast battlefield, stretching from Noyon in the south to Croisilles in the north—seven miles south-east of Arras. If the line fell back on both sides of this comparatively small frontage of the Somme (as it actually did) it would be almost impossible to hold on, and certainly would have been most unsound not to withdraw in time.

The junction with the French was quite secure at the time this order was issued. If it was intended that touch with the French must be maintained even in the case of their falling back south and south-westwards to cover Paris, it was not very clear, and in that case it might have entailed an effort by the Fifth Army to stretch still further its already thin and over-extended line, for even armies have a definite limit to their elasticity !

To keep in touch with the main British Army and to cover its right and Amiens was undoubtedly the correct course for the Fifth Army to pursue. The only movement for which Péronne could have formed a pivot was an offensive swing-forward of the Third Army against the right wing of the German attack, but, as things then were, such a manœuvre was out of the question. The Third Army was not able to do anything to maintain Péronne as a pivot, and it does not appear that G.H.Q. put any further pressure on it to do so.

It was early this afternoon that Haig came round and saw me, as I have already mentioned. But this visit did not take the place of a General Staff conference, which was badly needed.

The Fifth Army had now been exposed to three days of continuous fighting and of constant movement both by day and night without relief or any fresh support, except on the right in the III Corps area, where three French divisions had just begun to appear in the fighting-line, and one British division (8th) in the area of the XIX Corps. These French divisions belonged to General Pellé's V Corps, of Humbert's Third Army. Two of them, the 1st Dismounted Cavalry and the 9th, arrived behind the III Corps front on this evening, but they could not get into action till Sunday, the 24th, and Pellé arranged with Butler that on arrival they should relieve our 18th and 14th Divisions.

As these reinforcements came into line, the command passed to the French, and thus by Sunday our III Corps front came under the orders of the French Third Army. This shortened my front, and was an important relief to the Fifth Army Staff, for a front of over forty miles, exposed as it was along nearly its entire length to the fluctuations incidental to a violent battle, was more than one Army Staff could properly supervise. The Fifth Army was fighting two armies—Hutier's and Marwitz's, each of which was considerably more powerful than itself—while on its extreme right, south of the Oise, possibilities of attack by a third, Boehn's Seventh, could not be ruled out.

Now that the French were coming up, I hoped to pull out my III Corps and its divisions gradually, and to concentrate them behind my centre for the support, from my own resources, of the overstrained troops there. I could hope for little from elsewhere.

But the French did not part with a man or a gun of mine for many days, and on the 28th, when I handed over my command to General Rawlinson, Butler was still away with the French, and, though Maxse was co-operating closely with the Fifth Army, he was still supposed to be under French orders.

Casualties by now had been so heavy that in some cases two or three brigades were organized into one, and battalions were concentrated as companies ; yet all the time the frontage remained the same, and so did the pressure of the German attack. It placed a terrific strain on the moral and physical stamina of the men of Britain who composed the Fifth Army. The frequent gaps which inevitably occurred as the line got thinner and thinner brought a further severe strain on officers and men, who were always finding their flanks turned, having to make sudden counter-attacks to clear them, or to throw back a defensive flank, and finally to retire across the open under close and heavy fire.

But they never broke ; desperate, grim resolution, and a dogged courage characterized them all.

IV [1]

Sunday,
March 24. When Sunday morning broke on the fourth day of the struggle, the situation was critical ; our

[1] See Sketch Map 4, facing p. 120.

task was still unfinished, and the question was becoming more poignant : how much longer would the officers and men be able to stand the tremendous strain ? Certainly three fresh French divisions had taken over the front of our III Corps, and the 8th Division had arrived and was now holding the line of the Somme on the front of the XIX Corps, and it had repulsed several German attempts to force a crossing during the night. But the Germans also had received reinforcements, in even greater numbers. The odds against us were heavier than the first day, taking into consideration the fatigue of our men and the severe losses the units had suffered.

The French did not take the divisions of the III Corps out of the battle, but placed them in supporting positions, while the remnants of our 14th Division (III Corps), now under the orders of General Greenly, with some of the cavalry, still held the left of the French front. The very critical position of the 36th Division on the right of the XVIII Corps, facing in three directions, still continued, and the menace of a German advance southwards from Ham had become more accentuated, threatening both this division and the three French divisions still holding the line well to the east.

The Germans north of the Oise attacked the III French on the old III Corps front early in the morning from the direction of the Crozat Canal. Though our Allies were but freshly arrived, they

were in retreat by 9 a.m. and the roads in rear
began to get terribly congested with retiring
transport, guns and troops. The French Staff
work was not particularly good, the divisions
arriving being extremely ill-equipped, short of
even ball ammunition, as well as of their transport
and artillery.

Lee, commanding the 18th Division, at once
deployed his division on the line Caillouel–
Beaugies to cover the French retirement, and
held up the German infantry till 9 in the evening
with some French on his right and left. Further
retirements of the French then exposed Lee's left,
and at midnight he withdrew about three miles
through the French, where he was again in close
support of them.

The French fell back seven or eight miles
during the day, and our 14th Division, falling
back also, deployed on several occasions to cover
their retirement. Eventually the division crossed
the Canal du Nord, north of Noyon, during the
night and took up a position to hold the Canal
behind the French.

XVIII
Corps.
The French 10th Division had arrived the
previous evening—but without artillery—and by
Sunday morning it had occupied a position south
of Ham in rear of the right of the XVIII Corps,
facing north and north-eastwards. Before night
this division was involved in the general retirement and eventually occupied the left of the new
French line, which stretched' south-westwards

114

from the Canal du Nord to Abbécourt on the Oise—a distance of about twelve or thirteen miles. Behind the left of the XVIII Corps, two more divisions of the French II Cavalry Corps—62nd and 22nd—were beginning to arrive near Nesle during the day, but only a part of the 62nd came into line that evening on the Canal du Nord.

In spite of the very exposed position of the 36th Division it was not till the afternoon that it began to retire. On the extreme right near Cugny the 2nd R. Irish Rifles, finding itself practically cut off, just fought it out, heroically holding up the Germans for five hours and inflicting heavy losses on them, until its ammunition began to run out, when the battalion was finally overwhelmed. About this time a body of 150 cavalry made up from three different regiments, the Royals, 10th Hussars and 3rd Dragoon Guards, under General Harman, charged the Germans. They lost half their numbers, but they rode over a battalion of the German 5th Guard Division, killed or captured about 200, and took several machine guns. Some of our gallant infantry, exhausted and decimated as they were, jumped up on seeing this charge and rushed forward behind it, retaking some of the lost ground. This combined and gallant action stopped the German advance in this part of the field for a time.

During the night, the 36th Division was at last withdrawn behind the French for a short respite of rest and reorganization, though its artillery remained in action under the French, as their own had not yet come up. Further south the line of the Canal du Nord was held by our 14th Division in support to the French.

The centre and left of the XVIII Corps held the Somme west of Ham, where the attack was renewed at an early hour. The Germans gained a footing across the river at Canizy, but a counter-attack of three companies, by this time scarcely numbering 80 men, drove them back again for a time. By 10.30 a.m., however, the centre of the XVIII Corps had to fall back, and eventually took up a position on the Canal du Nord in touch with the left of the French, who had by then fallen back to their new line stretching from here southwards in front of Noyon to Abbécourt. Here the XVIII Corps was mixed up with the French 62nd Division, which by the evening was coming into line. The Germans came on towards the Canal du Nord behind our retreating men, but as they crossed the open ground our guns punished them heavily, in some cases remaining in position and firing till the enemy were within 800 yards.

The 20th Division was on the left of the XVIII Corps along the Somme. During the course of the day, its right flank exposed by the retirement of the rest of the Corps, it was also forced back to the line of the Canal du Nord after some hard fighting and several counter-attacks. During the day the 8th Division on its left was also driven off the Somme at Pargny, and a considerable gap occurred between these two divisions—in other words, between the XVIII and XIX Corps. The divisions on either side of this gap threw back their flanks north-west of Nesle to cover it as best they could during the night. ^{XIX Corps.}

Thus by dawn on Monday, the 25th, the Canal du Nord marked the front of the XVIII Corps, which had its left thrown back round Nesle. Southwards the line of the Canal was occupied by our 14th Division as a support to the French. Regarded as an obstacle the Canal du Nord was of little value, being unfinished and only flooded to the extent of about one foot deep of water.

Humbert's Third Army was now taking shape and he assumed command of the front as his divisions arrived, our British divisions being placed under his orders until they could be relieved, when they were to return to the Fifth Army. Maxse, however, kept a firm control over his own troops, and I kept in close touch with Maxse.

During these days I did not confine myself to using the telephone, but I motored over to see the Corps Commanders almost daily. I was thus able to learn not only the latest positions of the Corps but—what was almost more important— I could gauge their moral and physical condition as well. Such personal interviews enabled me to keep my finger on the pulse of my Army. I could see that everyone was now beginning to look drawn and tired, but there was still a confident, cheery manner everywhere. "We are killing an awful lot of the Boche," "even if we have to fall back, we will keep the line intact until reinforcements come up in sufficient numbers, and then we will have a go at him." Such was the tenor of the remarks made to me in the course of my visits. All the same, it was evident that we could not go on for ever, and that if the divisions and battalions were not "nursed," and if they were exposed too long to the onslaught of superior numbers, there would be a complete break.

The officers and men were playing their part in this desperate game splendidly, and I had to play mine, too ; this was to see, as far as I could, that units were not exposed to annihilation or to complete exhaustion, that flanks were not permanently exposed, nor gaps left too long unfilled. To continue the retreat was therefore still the right course to pursue, as it was the only one which could ensure keeping the line intact.

But I did not mean to give up the line of the Somme if I could help it ; indeed, G.H.Q. had issued orders that it was to be held " at all costs." In fact, the XIX Corps held on to it for two whole days—the 24th and 25th—and was not withdrawn till the French on the right had fallen back to Roye, seven miles to the west, and our Third Army on the left was retiring on the line Bray–Albert–the Ancre, eight miles and more behind that flank. To increase our difficulties, both colleagues on our flanks tended to retire away from us, as well as behind us, the French for several days falling back south-westwards to cover Paris, while the Third Army on this and the two following days was forced away westwards and sometimes even north-westwards.

Intending to hang on to the Somme as long as possible, I now thought the arrival of the French 22nd Division near Nesle offered a good opportunity for delivering a counter-attack in some force, to throw the Germans back across the Somme at Béthencourt and Pargny. Robillot commanded the French Corps here, and I had met him in 1913 when I attended the French manœuvres. He was an active, strong, thick-set little man and a well-trained officer; I hoped, therefore, for his whole-hearted co-operation. Late that evening I arranged with him, Maxse, and Watts, who all had to take part in this projected counter-attack, that the French 22nd Division would attack northwards from the direction of Nesle, and part of our 8th and 24th Divisions south-eastwards, in order to regain the line of the Somme about Pargny early next morning, converging on the Germans from two directions.

The hour was fixed for 8 a.m. on the 25th, but when the time came the French were not near the position; in fact they had not advanced beyond Billancourt, about two miles south of Nesle. The hour was postponed till 11 a.m. By then the French 22nd Division was retreating and the

Germans attacking us heavily, so the counter-attack as arranged never came off. When Maxse protested to Robillot because the 22nd Division was not ready at the hour arranged, and never moved forward at all to the attack, Robillot replied, "*Mais, ce n'etait qu'un projet!*" One cannot always be sure that "*projets*" will turn into facts when working with Allies!

But to return to Sunday, the 24th. Some very severe fighting took place also opposite the right of the 8th Division (XIX Corps) during the day. Here the battalions of this division, and eventually those of the 20th Division (XVIII Corps) on its right, as already stated, were driven from the line of the Somme at Béthencour tand Pargny. Several fierce counter-attacks were made, but though they checked and delayed the Germans very considerably, there was never enough weight in them to throw back the enemy to the far side of the river, and before nightfall the Germans had penetrated about a couple of miles from the Somme, forcing their way between the two Corps (XVIII and XIX). On the rest of the XIX Corps front for seven or eight miles as far north as Péronne our troops successfully resisted all attempts of the Germans to force a passage of the river.

Though the fighting had been severe on my right, the presence of the French afforded me some relief, and the responsibilities there were gradually being transferred to their shoulders.

MARCH 24TH AND 25TH 1918. SKETCH MAP 4.

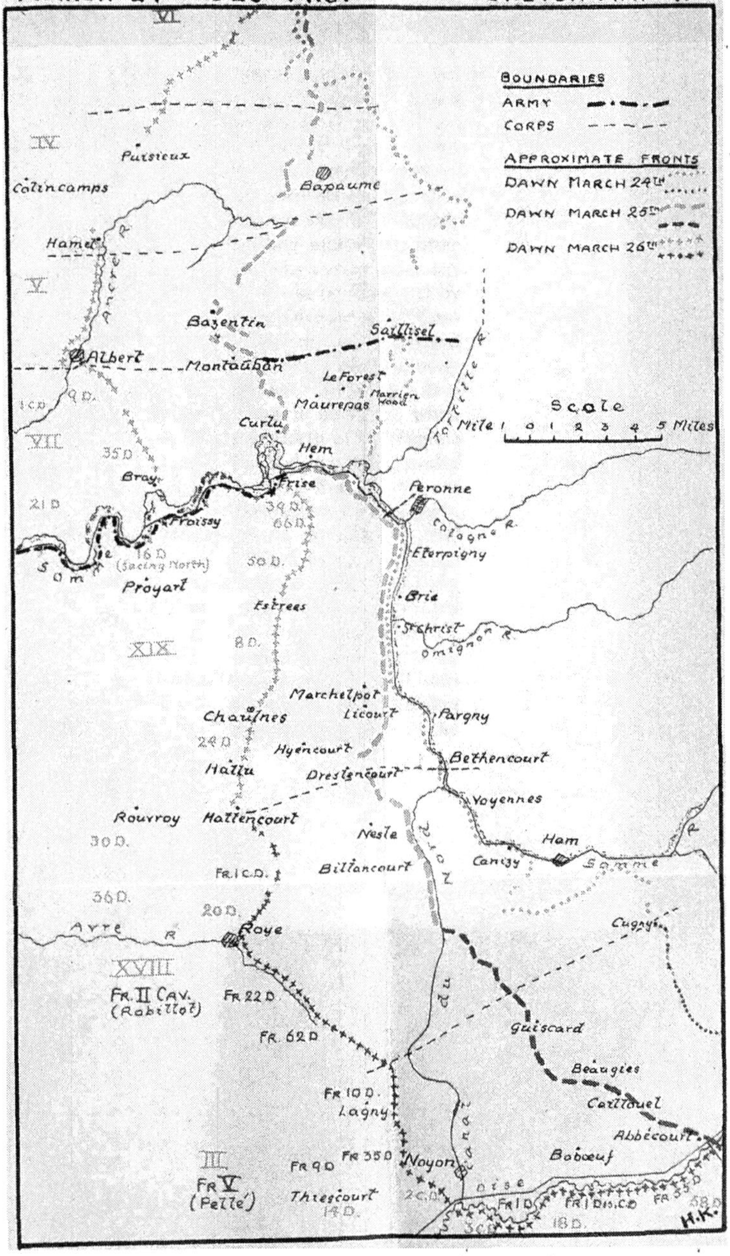

It was towards the left that anxieties were now VII
being principally felt: the pressure exerted by Corps.
Von der Marwitz's Army had been increasing in
that direction, and Congreve was finding great
difficulty in maintaining touch with the Third
Army. The boundary between the two Armies
ran rather south-west, but the V Corps of the
Third Army was compelled by superior force to
retire westwards, and even north-westwards, thus
ever widening the gap between us. By Saturday
evening Congreve was holding more than three
miles of the Third Army front in a vain endeavour
to fill the gap. Though it could be ill spared by
Watts, I sent the 1st Cavalry Division up to Congreve early on Sunday morning, as a mounted
cavalry force was essential to cover his constantly
exposed and moving left flank. Before two days
had passed, I wished I had it back, for when
Congreve and all his troops north of the Somme
were placed under the Third Army, this cavalry
division passed to it also. The Somme did not
prove to be a good boundary between the Armies,
and was no improvement on an arbitrary line
drawn on the map. The Third Army, during the
following days, fell back several miles behind my
left and did not destroy the bridges or post any
troops to hold them, and it carried Congreve's
VII Corps with it. A cavalry division under my
orders south of the Somme could have been
moved quickly to meet this unexpected situation
and would have saved many commanders in the

Fifth Army, including myself, some extremely harrowing moments of anxiety, and the lives of a good many of our men.

I had passed on the order that the line of the Somme and the Tortille northwards was to be held at all costs, in accordance with orders received from G.H.Q. ; but this was not possible, and Congreve realized that he would have to fall back. He therefore decided early in the day on a second position and issued orders for its occupation in case of necessity. Behind and south of the Somme, near Péronne, his line was held with comparative ease, but north of the river, which here turned west again, very heavy fighting was experienced during the day. By 12 (noon) the remnants of the 21st Division had been driven back a distance of two miles to the spurs in front of Hem and Maurepas.

The 35th Division was now arriving and this had been placed under Congreve's orders. The leading two battalions of the first brigade, after a night-march of over ten miles, were now ordered forward to retake the lost ground. As our battalions went forward the Germans were advancing also, but when they saw our men they turned round and fell back, taking up a defensive position. The advance of these battalions stopped the Germans in this part of the field till 5 p.m., and a fight at close range ensued, during which the Germans suffered heavy casualties. Then our men retired under orders to a position in rear, which by now was held by the rest of the 35th Division, and what remained of the 21st was withdrawn for rest and reorganization.

Further to the left the 9th Division held the line as far north as Saillisel—three miles inside the Third Army front. On its right stood the South African Brigade under General F. Dawson. The Divisional Commander had told him the night before that the line was to be held " at all costs," and this he and his brigade, now reduced to 500 men, determined to do.

By 9 a.m. the Germans attacked him and by 10 a.m. the troops on both flanks began to retire. By 11 a.m. the Germans, having set fire to the grass, got up under cover of the smoke to within 200 yards of the South Africans, but here they were held. By 3 p.m. the Germans had seized a village (Le Forest) in their rear. During all this time the gallant band had been subjected to a heavy bombardment. At 4.30 p.m. the Germans brought up three fresh battalions and overwhelmed it, reduced as it then was to 100 men. In this gallant defence some parties of the 21st Division had taken part. The position had been held for seven and a half hours, and the losses inflicted on the Germans had been very heavy. It is difficult to find words to express our debt to, and our admiration for, these brave men. Perhaps no better tribute can be paid them than to quote the sincere but simple praise of their foes. In one of their regimental histories these words are found : " during the afternoon the 357th and 237th Reserve Regiments captured Marrière Wood in spite of the heroic and desperate defence of the almost completely destroyed South African Brigade."

While this splendid stand was being made by the men of South Africa on the left of the Army, some forty miles away on the right a battalion of Irishmen, the 2nd R. Irish Rifles, as has already been stated, had also fought to the last and was overwhelmed after five hours. Many desperate counter-attacks had also been made by men from the homeland along the whole front.

Are we not justified in seeing a deep significance in the fact that such endurance, courage and self-sacrifice was being displayed this day by men who came from homes many thousands of miles apart? Surely there is something in the spirit of the race that binds all the peoples who come within its fold into a great brotherhood? Surely we can preserve this great thing? The words of the Eton boating song come back to me : " And nothing on earth shall sever the chain that is round us now." The principal links in that chain seem to me to be a sense of duty, and a generous sympathy for each other, wherever we come from. As long as those characteristics mark the people of this Empire, I do not fear its disruption.

    .   .   .   .   .   .

The annihilation of the South African Brigade

now reduced the 9th Division to two brigades only. These two brigades, hammered, battered, and exhausted after four days and nights of fighting, fell back during the day about five miles. Here the 35th Division, just arrived, had established the front, reinforced and supported by " Hunt's Force." This was one of many of our extemporized formations which necessity forced upon us. It was formed, by Congreve's orders, of his Corps reinforcements, consisting of unfit men, recruits who had never been in battle, men back from leave, men at courses of instruction, etc. Colonel Hunt, with great energy, organized all these men in the course of a day into eight battalions, supplied them as best he could with machine guns, Lewis guns, etc., which he salved from other units, and then brought these improvised battalions forward into the battle.

The right of the Third Army during the day fell back about eight miles, and that night it was established at Bazentin-le-Petit, behind our left and with a gap of over two miles between the two Armies. Into this gap Congreve thrust the 1st Cavalry Division with its left back thrown back north of Montauban.

Meanwhile Congreve's right, the 39th Division, still held the Somme behind Péronne, and as his left fell back, this division and what remained of the 16th took up a line further west along the Somme facing north to protect his flank here along this part of the river. These troops were not seriously attacked on this day, but they could see the German forces pushing on north of the river, and fired heavily into their flank.

The original plan of the German High Command had been to employ Hutier's Army to hold the line of the Crozat Canal, and the Somme as far as Péronne, as a protection to hold off the French, while the rest of their forces was to drive back the British north of the Somme, cut them from the French and press their right back towards the sea. This, however, had been considerably modified. Hutier was under the orders of the Crown Prince, who, finding that he was getting on, persuaded the High Command to reinforce him. The majority of the German reserves, therefore, were sent to their left flank against the Fifth Army and the French, and not against our Third Army. The result was that when the gap was created on Monday and Tuesday, the 25th and 26th, north of Albert and the Ancre in the front of the Third Army, there were insufficient German reserves near by to exploit it. If Ludendorff had kept to his original plan, the consequences for the British would have been grave. I could not know any of these plans at the time, however, nor had I time to think of much more than the immediate dangers facing the Fifth Army.

That afternoon I went out to see Watts and

Congreve. As I passed near a Divisional Headquarters I looked in about 5.30 p.m. and found the General so weary that he could hardly keep his eyes open. I do not think he had had four hours' sleep in three nights and days. I made his A.D.C. promise to make him lie down and not disturb him for two hours and then see that a good dinner was ready for him.

I then passed on to see Congreve, who was in a small canvas hut on the north bank of the Somme. When I walked in he was speaking on the telephone to one of his divisions and I waited till he had finished. I heard him say, " I don't care a damn, it has got to be done ! "

He then turned and saw me, and said, " Hullo, is that you ? " There was no lack of nerve, energy or courage in his keen, smiling eyes, and his determined spirit was typical of his gallant and hard-pressed Corps.

v

Very early in the morning, before 2 a.m., Monday, orders arrived from G.H.Q. placing all the troops March 25. north of the Somme, with VII Corps Headquarters, under the Third Army, and at the same time informing me that it had now been arranged that the French should take over up to that river, under General Fayolle, who was commanding the group of armies in that area. The Fifth Army was thus cut off from G.H.Q. as regards military operations, and G.H.Q. gave up all responsibilities for the British troops under my command south of the Somme.

The line of the Somme now made a clear line of demarcation between the Third Army and ourselves, and might therefore have helped to prevent gaps arising, but this arrangement in fact did not really benefit the Fifth Army, and the junction between the two Armies became daily more unsatisfactory. After all, it is better to make one unit responsible for both sides of a valley which runs at right angles to the front. In any case, it would have been better if Congreve with the VII Corps Staff had remained with the Fifth Army even if his troops north of the river were placed under the Third Army. All sorts of units were now being piled on to the XIX Corps, in my endeavours to reinforce and help it. As I managed to get back troops from the French belonging to the III and XVIII Corps, these were sent to reinforce the XIX Corps, together with many extemporized formations, and before Wednesday General Watts had some nineteen different units under his orders and administration. This was far more than one Staff could properly handle. Staff work would have been infinitely easier if the XIX Corps front had been divided between it and the VII Corps.

Placing the Fifth Army under Fayolle's group of armies made no material difference. He issued no orders to me, and I only saw him once for a few minutes.

It may have been in Haig's mind that by getting the French to be responsible for the line up to the Somme he could more easily induce Pétain to keep in touch with the British Army rather than to retire south-west to cover Paris, as he was already commencing to do.

By Monday morning the French had become responsible for the ground lately occupied by the right of the Fifth Army, and Humbert of their Third Army assumed command. By now he had two Corps, the V under General Pellé and the II Cavalry under General Robillot. French Third Army.

A general account of events in this area will enable the reader to follow the course of the battle and the situation of the Fifth Army as it was affected by the French on our right.

On this Monday morning Pellé's Corps consisted of four French divisions, the 9th, 1st Dismounted Cavalry, 10th and 55th, the two latter having arrived the previous day. These were holding a line from Abbécourt on the Oise, running north-westwards behind Guiscard for ten miles where they connected with Robillot's Corps and our XVIII Corps. Behind the French, under Pellé's orders, were the British 18th and 14th Divisions and the 2nd and 3rd Cavalry Divisions, in positions of close support. Robillot's Corps, mixed with the divisions of our XVIII Corps, carried the line on to the Canal du Nord. The line then ran northwards along the Canal as far as the east of Nesle, where it was swung

back about a mile round the north of the little
town in order to meet the situation which had
been created by the German success of the previous evening, when they had forced back the left
of the XVIII Corps and the right of the XIX
Corps from the Somme at Voyennes, Béthencourt
and Pargny.

French
V Corps.
The Germans early drove a hole into Pellé's
line, and he retired the centre of his Corps about
three miles, thus creating a dangerous re-entrant,
his right having the Oise close behind it. The
Germans were quick to take advantage of this,
and about 1 p.m. attacked Pellé's right from the
north. By 5 p.m. they had driven it south across
the Oise. Two more French divisions, the 1st
and 35th, arrived during the day, and with the
help of these Pellé maintained his centre in front
of Noyon for some time, but his left fell back
behind the Canal du Nord and did not stop till
it reached Lagny, two miles west of the Canal.
Pellé than issued orders withdrawing his right
behind the Oise and his centre and left behind
Noyon.

Meanwhile our 18th Division, which was holding a line in support of Pellé's right, had been
attacked and was fighting hard before 11 a.m.
By 3.30 p.m. the orders to retire south across
the Oise were received, but General Sadleir-
Jackson, commanding a brigade of the division,
seeing that the retirement of the French on his
left would be difficult, launched a counter-attack

at 5.30 p.m. against the village of Babœuf, which had been seized by the Germans. His brigade had come through five days' continuous fighting and was greatly reduced in numbers, but within half an hour it retook Babœuf, captured 10 machine guns, and killed or captured 230 Germans, and retained its position till 2 a.m. next day, when it crossed the Oise and rejoined its division, now concentrated under orders from the French ten miles south-east of Noyon : thence it passed completely out of Butler's control for many days.

Our 14th Division, which started the day by holding the Canal du Nord north of Noyon, in support of the French, was involved also in some rear-guard fighting in the evening as the left of Pellé's Corps fell back past it, and during the night it was also withdrawn southwards under French orders six miles west of Noyon.

Our cavalry under Harman had been pushed forward north of the 14th Division, to cover the retreat of the French, and it held the line of the Canal du Nord till the early hours of the following day.

The 2nd and 3rd Cavalry Divisions were concentrated once again during this day, and by nightfall they also were withdrawn three to four miles south of Noyon.

Thus, during Monday, Pellé's Corps, now consisting of six French and three very attenuated British divisions, had been driven back and retired about eight miles, partly due south and partly south-westwards—towards Paris and away from the Fifth Army! Tuesday morning found his Corps in a half-circle, with Noyon about two and a half miles in front of its centre.

These dispositions had drawn the whole of the III Corps away from the Fifth Army—the 18th, the 14th and the two Cavalry Divisions finding themselves by the evening either south of the Oise or west of Noyon.

The French Command, though it quite properly commanded our troops when on the actual battle front, had no right to withdraw them in this direction to cover Paris. The understanding was that as the French took over our line our troops should be relieved as early as possible and sent back to the Fifth Army. I was counting on them, and frequently sent messages to Humbert and also to Anthoine, of Marshal Pétain's Staff, asking for my divisions back. It was weak of Butler and an error of judgment to allow his divisions to be moved in these directions, and he should certainly not have consented to it without my knowledge and approval.

Maxse's conduct under similar circumstances was very different. He retained a firm hold over his troops, and though readily and willingly co-operating with the French, he was careful to remain an integral part of the Fifth Army and keep as closely in touch with me as circumstances would admit.

It is interesting to reflect what would have been the result of the day on the front of Pellé's Corps if it had been held by an equal number of British divisions. The front held in the morning was ten miles—a front covered by less than two divisions of the Fifth Army on the 21st of March when they were attacked by overwhelming numbers of fresh and confident Germans. By Sunday the German troops were already showing signs of weariness. When one sees what barely 300 tired men of Sadleir-Jackson's brigade were capable of doing at Babœuf, it is by no means outside the bounds of possibility that six comparatively fresh British divisions would have thrown the German attack back on this part of the battlefield. As it was, the repercussion of the retreat of Pellé's Corps was felt along my whole line, as far north as Péronne.

Further north, on Pellé's left, stood the French 62nd Division of Robillot's Corps, and the line was carried on round Nesle by our 30th, 20th and 61st Divisions, all under the orders of Robillot. French II Cav. Corps.

In the morning, the gap between our XVIII and XIX Corps north of Nesle still existed. It had been my intention to rectify this by attacking the Germans and driving them back to the line of the Somme about Pargny. The fresh French division, the 22nd, was to play the main part in this action, as has been already recounted, and the attack was timed to take place at 8 a.m. The French first asked that the counter-attack

133

should be postponed till 11 a.m., but as a matter of fact the 22nd Division had never come forward at all and remained south of Nesle. Long before that hour the Germans were attacking vigorously in an endeavour to exploit the gap between the two Corps.

The 24th Division, XIX Corps, through a misunderstanding, was also late in coming up to fill the gap as had been intended, and when it advanced it found the Germans already northwest of Nesle.

XVIII Corps.

The German attack therefore fell only on the thin line of tired troops belonging to our 61st and 20th Divisions, but they covered Nesle for some three hours and did not retire till 11 a.m. when they fell back to Billancourt, about one and a half miles south of Nesle, where the French 22nd Division was found. The left of our troops holding the Canal du Nord was now turned, but in spite of this the Scottish Rifles on the extreme left held on till 2 p.m., very few of them surviving. The rest of the Canal du Nord was covered by the British 20th and 30th Divisions for three miles southwards and was successfully held till nearly 5 p.m., when the French 62nd Division on their right was driven off the Canal. Both flanks of these two divisions on the Canal were thus exposed and they had to retire. But the Germans were close on our men, and they could not get away without some fierce counter-attacks and heavy casualties.

Eventually, as evening came on, our divisions were withdrawn behind the French 62nd and 22nd Divisions, and—contrary to French instructions—owing to Maxse's firm orders—all his divisions were concentrated westwards in the neighbourhood of Roye.

Meanwhile Robillot's Corps continued its retirement south-westwards during the night, and by Tuesday morning it was standing on the line Lagny–Roye facing north-east, having fallen back during the previous twenty-four hours a distance of about seven miles.

Maxse's firmness and decision in keeping his Corps together and moving it westwards and north-westwards saved the Fifth Army, and in fact the whole British Army and the Allied cause, from a disaster : for a complete separation of the French and British Armies would have been nothing else.

While all this was going on, the XIX Corps was struggling to maintain itself on the Somme. Its right flank was already thrown back from St. Christ towards Licourt to guard against the irruption of the Germans across the river at Pargny. Its left flank was uncovered by the retirement of the Third Army, whose line, Curlu–Bazentin-le-Petit–west of Bapaume, was already four miles behind it. XIX Corps.

Nevertheless it was not till late in the evening that orders for a retirement of four miles were issued. The counter-attack to re-establish the right of the Corps on the Somme was never carried out, as we have seen.

The 24th Division was moving up to support the counter-attack of the 8th Division and fill the gap between it and the French, when it found the Germans in occupation of Dreslin-court; the enemy at once began pressing this division, but were successfully held till the after-noon. The pressure and the casualties were heavy, and eventually the division fell back after dark to Hattencourt–Hallu. Here some reinforce-ments in the shape of three extemporized bat-talions were sent up by Maxse to the 24th and proved very useful.

About 8 a.m. the Germans had also attacked the 8th Division, and by 10.30 had taken Licourt, though two companies of Yorkshires bravely defended it to the last. By 1 p.m., after con-tinuous heavy fighting, the 8th Division held Hyencourt and Marchelpot, in touch with the 24th on its right and with its left still holding the Somme at St. Christ.

St. Christ was held till late in the evening, when the Germans, still pressing our line back from the south, made the position untenable, and our men had to fight their way back.

Further north, the enemy, under cover of a heavy machine-gun and artillery fire, gradually established a footing on our bank of the Somme at Eterpigny on the 66th Division front. Captain Toye, commanding a company of the Middlesex, held on here till he was surrounded. With 10 men left he fought his way out, then collected 70 more of another battalion and led his party back to our new line. For this very determined and gallant action he was awarded the V.C.

Watts now felt the position of the XIX Corps was becoming impossible, and he was right. He spoke to me on the telephone, and I authorized a withdrawal of four miles after dark, to a new line —Hattencourt–Chaulnes–Estrées–Frise (on the Somme), where we hoped to obtain touch with the Third Army. There were now six divisions under his command, but hardly one of them could muster more than 1000 rifles, and his front was thirteen or fourteen miles long, with both flanks exposed.

About 11.30 that evening we heard from the VII Corps that the Third Army was retiring again during the night to the line Bray–Albert–the Ancre. This would place the Third Army once more five miles behind our left at Frise, but according to the G.H.Q. orders fixing the Somme as the boundary, it was supposed to be responsible for the line of the river. Nevertheless we took steps to guard the river-crossings ourselves, between our new front at Frise and Bray, and this duty was allotted to the 16th Division. VII Corps.

The line of the Somme about Brie was still held by the XIX Corps at 6 p.m., and the general retirement to the new line commenced after dark. About three companies of the Middlesex never XIX Corps.

retired, but fought it out. The rest of the battalion, covered by a rear-guard composed of its own commanding officer, Lt.-Colonel Page, and some of his battalion Staff, only got away just in time. By dawn next morning the new line was occupied, but both flanks were still in danger, the French holding a thin and very shaky line on our right and the Third Army being once more five miles behind the left.

To meet possible developments resulting from this situation, we issued Army orders to the XIX Corps at 10 p.m., to the effect that if it was heavily pressed it was to fall back fighting to a line Rouvroy–Proyart–Froissy, which would bring the Fifth Army back into line with the Third Army, and during the night the XIX Corps issued orders to some entrenching battalions and engineers to commence fortifying this line.

The Third Army.

It was during this Monday and the previous night that the Third Army gave up Bapaume and fell back behind the Ancre and north of it, a distance in places of over ten miles. A very dangerous situation developed on its front during this afternoon. Its IV Corps (General Harper), although it consisted of six divisions, left a gap of four miles in its line, from Hamel to the north of Puisieux, which was some twelve miles north of the left flank of the Fifth Army. Into this gap the Germans had penetrated to a depth of three miles, and had seized Colincamps before nightfall. Colincamps is barely nineteen miles north-east of Amiens. At the same time the Fifth Army was still holding off the Germans on the Somme at Brie—twenty-three miles from Amiens.

That the Germans did not exploit this great advantage which they had won was due to the fact that they had comparatively few divisions concentrated against the Third Army owing to their reinforcements having already been sent to their left and centre under Hutier and Marwitz. It was fortunate for us that this was so. To have rolled up Byng's right wing from the north and advanced on Amiens would not only have cut the British Army from the French, but would have enabled the enemy to destroy the right wing of the Third Army.

Although the Fifth Army was echeloned several miles to the east in front of the Third Army, and in that position was the best possible protection to its right, it seems that G.H.Q. was possessed with the fear that the chief danger lay to the south of the Third Army, and issued orders that troops should hold the line of the river facing south, and at one time the 1st Cavalry Division was directed to take up such a front. In reality, the danger to the Third Army lay to the north, on its own centre and left, inasmuch as the Germans were already in Colincamps, and actually the Fifth Army was the one which required protection along the Somme—from the north !

G.H.Q. at this time undoubtedly under-estimated the Fifth Army, what it had done, and what it was still capable of doing, to stay the attack of the Germans, and to exhaust their divisions, in spite of the terrific strain imposed on its troops. Such a misapprehension was due, at least in part, to the lack of personal contact maintained between G.H.Q. and me. The state of mind existing there was such that the Fifth Army was now entirely discounted, the Third Army was looked on as the right of the British Army, and the danger of it being turned, driven north of Amiens and completely cut off from the French, took sole possession of the General Staff mind. But the situation was not as bad as all that. The Fifth Army still existed, and the Germans had still to take it seriously into account. As long as it remained in being south of the Somme, the right of the Third Army was safe. Even by this Monday evening the Germans were becoming worn and spent. Before the shattered remnants of the Fifth Army were withdrawn from the battlefield, the German prospects of final victory were gone, the War was lost for them, if it was not quite over.

Indications exist that G.H.Q. regarded even the line of the Ancre as merely a rear-guard position, and were contemplating further retirements.

Two days later the Third Army left the bridges over the Somme unguarded, permitting the

Germans to cross to the south bank in rear of the overstrained men of the Fifth Army, still devotedly holding back the enemy after seven days and nights of continuous fighting.

It was during the afternoon of this Monday—the 25th—that the momentous conference at Doullens took place. All the Army Commanders were present except myself. Considering how little G.H.Q. knew of the situation and moral of the Fifth Army, it was unfortunate that I was not there, as I could have thrown some light on the real situation of the Germans, the Fifth Army, and the French. It could not have been that G.H.Q. thought the position on my front required my unremitting attention, for Byng was present, and the situation of his Army with the enemy pressing into Colincamps, if not already in actual possession of it, was one to cause even more anxiety and demand more immediate attention than that on the Fifth Army front.

Not only was I not summoned to this conference at Doullens, but I was not even informed that it had taken place, and I knew nothing about it till months afterwards.

The only indication that reached me of its deliberations and conclusions was that on Tuesday I received a brief message telling me that Marshal Foch had been appointed Generalissimo and that, as he would visit my Head-quarters in the afternoon, I was to stay in to meet him. But I will return to this later. It was during this

Monday afternoon that we organized under the Staff of the Army a body which later attained some notoriety as " Carey's Force."

This force consisted of everyone we could collect, and included electrical and mechanical engineers—surveyors—500 men of the U.S. Engineers—tunnellers and miners—Army, Corps and Sniping Schools—signallers. The Army Signal School supplied its communications, 9 grooms acted as mounted orderlies, and it was equipped with some wagons and lorries for transport work.

The total strength of the force amounted to just over 2000 men, and for the moment I put General P. G. Grant, who was my Chief Engineer, in command, and gave him two officers of our Army Staff to assist him. When General Carey returned from leave on Tuesday afternoon (26th) I directed him to take command to set General Grant free to attend to his proper functions.

This force was deployed eventually along the line of the old Amiens defences east of Villers-Bretonneux, which I had rescued from demolition in December when the Fifth Army first arrived on this front.

Carey's Force was not the only force of this nature which was organized in the Fifth Army, though it is the best known to the public— principally due to the statements made by Mr. Lloyd George in the House of Commons. Congreve had already organized Hunt's force of eight battalions, as already mentioned. Watts

142

in the XIX Corps had also organized a number of reinforcing units from any available troops, such as men at schools, reinforcement camps, stragglers, etc. In his report he writes : " This procedure was continued. These units were pushed forward to divisions in accordance with urgent demands, and they were undoubtedly of great value in restoring the situation at critical points. It is possible that as time went on they added a certain amount to the disorganization which inevitably took place, but they did good work."

Maxse also had organized similar units and he had sent three of these improvised battalions to reinforce the 24th Division, XIX Corps, during the day, as I have previously mentioned.

Late in the afternoon I went over to see Maxse and Watts. Maxse's Head-quarters had just been bombed, but the absence of his artillery was all that was worrying him. I found him very indignant with the French, for though they had sent his divisions back, they had taken all his artillery south-westwards with them. This roused me also, and I wrote Humbert a sharp letter demanding the immediate return of our guns. On my way back I saw the sad, but rather familiar, tragedy of civilians, chiefly women, in a retreat, trudging down the road, and picked up several of them and gave them a lift on their way.

The atmosphere behind our lines was full of

143

wild rumours : everyone except the speaker was
" running away " ; the Germans were already
through our line and behind us ; German officers
dressed in British uniforms were said to be going
about telling everyone that all was lost and that
they should retreat at once. It recalled the
days of August 1914. Not a quarter of the
stories were true, and I never heard that we
caught a single German behind our lines in
British uniform.

These inventions did not remain altogether
in the area of the Fifth Army—they floated back
much further, growing in volume as they went.
They acquired fine proportions by the time they
reached G.H.Q., but they attained their full
stature only on arrival in London ! It was a
strange anomaly—the nearer the front line, the
greater the feeling of confidence : the only signs
of panic were to be found well behind our front,
at Doullens, and in London !

VI [1]

Tuesday,
March 26.

The French now held the south bank of the
Oise as far as Noyon, but this front was not
attacked. On the right of the battle, from the
Oise northwards, Pellé's V Corps held a line,
its right on Mont Renaud and its left north of
Lagny, a front of about five miles. The remnants
of our 14th Division and our 2nd Cavalry Division
were in reserve and represented what remained

[1] See Sketch Map 5, facing p. 168.

144

of our III Corps : the 58th Division was holding III
most of its original front south of the Oise, while Corps.
the 18th and 3rd Cavalry Divisions were between
five and ten miles south of Noyon, behind the
Oise, and were no longer under Butler's control.

North of Pellé stood Robillot's Corps, with the
62nd, 22nd and 1st Cavalry Divisions.

Maxse's XVIII Corps was on the left rear XVIII
north-west of Roye, and it was fortunate its Corps.
divisions were so placed, for they were thus able
to fill the big gap of five miles on the right of
our XIX Corps which the retirement of the two
French Corps seven to ten miles southwards and
south-westwards created.

From Hattencourt, five miles north of Roye, XIX
where rested the left of Robillot's command, Corps.
consisting of his own and Maxse's Corps, Watts's
XIX Corps stretched to the Somme at Frise, a
front of thirteen miles. With the Third Army
four miles in its rear at Bray, this was now the
main part of the Fifth Army's front ; but it could
not be held for long, with both its neighbours
falling back behind it and away from it.

The Germans began their attacks at 6 a.m.
this day on the centre of Robillot's Corps in
front of Roye and to the east of it, and by 11 a.m.
they had captured the town, the French falling
back some three miles, almost due south.

About this hour a new French Corps (the
VI) began to arrive west of Roye, but actually
only its 5th Cavalry Division appeared. This

division, however, helped to fill the gap between the left of Robillot and the right of Maxse, for by nightfall the former's Corps had been driven five miles south-westwards, thus ever widening the gap between the French and the Fifth Army.

French V Corps.

Meanwhile Pellé's Corps, on the right of the battlefield, was also attacked at an early hour and began to give ground. In consequence, our 2nd and 3rd Cavalry Divisions, under Generals Pitman and Harman, were ordered forward, and with considerable skill, mobility and much steadfast gallantry, held almost the whole of the French line of this Corps for some six hours, and only fell back after 4 p.m. when the French on their left (uncovered in turn on their left flank by the retirement of Robillot's Corps) began falling back.

By 6 p.m. Pellé's Corps was established on its new line, having pivoted on its right on Mont Renaud, which it had held throughout the day, while its left fell back a distance of about five miles. The Corps was thus facing almost north when day broke next morning. The British troops in this part of the field were now again in reserve : the 18th and 3rd Cavalry Divisions south of the Oise, the 14th and 2nd Cavalry Divisions being in billets some five miles south-west of Thiescourt, behind the centre of Pellé's front.

The 14th Division, which had commenced the battle with an infantry strength of only 190

146

officers and 5737 men, had already lost in the
desperate and continuous fighting 128 officers
and 4261 men. Other divisions in the Fifth
Army may not have suffered quite so severely,
but these figures are not far from average ones
and will enable the reader to grasp the extent
of the sacrifice made by these men in fulfilling
the task which was set them.

We must now return to Maxse and his four XVIII
divisions, all safely under his own command, Corps.
near Roye and westwards—except for the artillery,
both field and heavy, all of which had been
carried off under orders of the French to support
them as they moved south. Thus the unfortunate
men of this Corps were exposed to the attack of
the German guns and infantry without one single
gun to cover them during the whole day's hard
fighting, which was the sixth they had been
called on to undertake. It is no wonder that
I had found Maxse the previous evening in no
sweet and gentle mood !

Maxse's first orders were to establish a line
with the right on the Avre and the left at Rouvroy,
a front of about five miles, to which latter place
the right of the XIX Corps was retiring. This
line was to be occupied by the 36th on the right,
and the 30th on the left ; before the 36th could
reach its positions, however, it found the enemy
already in them, having early driven the French
out of Roye.

The Germans, fortunately, did not seem inclined to attack, in spite of immunity from artillery fire, and it was not till after dark that they advanced, when they took part of our line ; but a counter-attack threw them back, and our line here was successfully held throughout the day and the night. But a dangerous situation for the 36th now arose, for, owing to the Germans occupying its designated position, a gap was created between its right and the left of the neighbouring 30th Division. The enemy penetrated into this during the evening, temporarily cutting off two brigades of the 36th. On the left of Maxse's Corps no serious attack was made during the day, though a rear-guard of a hundred men of the Duke of Cornwall's Light Infantry, under the brigade major, held the village of Le Quesnoy, fighting desperately and coming more than once to the bayonet, until 6.30 p.m., when the few survivors fell back to our main position.

Meanwhile the artillery of this Corps had been covering and supporting Robillot's French Corps and had fallen back southwards with it, but during the night, partly owing to peremptory orders from Maxse, some of the batteries moved across towards Montdidier and came under the orders of their own Corps once again.

XIX Corps.

Owing to the position on both flanks the XIX Corps, now the main part of the Fifth Army, received orders early to fall back to a new line —Rouvroy–Rosières–Proyart–the Somme, where it was hoped a firm connexion with the Third Army would be established at Bray.

The Germans were attacking heavily by 8 a.m. and Watts's exposed right was turned and driven back, while the village of Herbécourt on his left was also captured. By the afternoon, under continuous pressure, but fighting steadily, the Corps had withdrawn and was established on its new line.

In the 24th Division, on Watts's right, a battalion of East Surreys did not get the order to retire till the Germans were within a hundred yards. It was then too late, and the C.O., seizing some old trenches, fought it out till ammunition was completely exhausted, when the Germans were able to capture the position and 2 officers and 55 unwounded men, the only survivors of the battalion. This is one more example of the heroic, the steadfast, the self-sacrificing spirit with which our men fought, worthy representatives of a great people.

During this day's retirement, another counter-attack was carried out by our tired men, when part of two battalions of the 50th Division—now at last under the command of their new General, H. C. Jackson—re-took most of Framerville and put a stop for the day to any further advance by the Germans from this direction.

On the extreme left, the 16th Division, terribly reduced, established the new line and beat off various attacks during the afternoon and evening, but its flank resting on the Somme was shot into and enfiladed from across the river, the Third Army having been pushed back about seven miles.

What was even more serious was the fact that the bridges had not been secured or destroyed. Thus the enemy could cross to the south bank and descend in the rear of the Fifth Army—which, in fact, he proceeded to do next day. There were no fresh reserves with which to meet this new threat on the left of the XIX Corps, and it was, in fact, very nearly the last straw. The reports of the retreat of the Third Army and of the unguarded bridges did not reach Watts until 9 in the evening, when he at once issued orders to destroy all the bridges as far west as Cerizy and called on the Fifth Army for help to meet this new danger.

To deal with it I had little under my hand, but fortunately Grant had organized his hetero-geneous force and it was already in position on the old Amiens defence line, about seven miles behind the XIX Corps front, and in touch with the right of the Third Army across the river.

We sent 300 men of this force, six Lewis guns, and a Canadian motor machine-gun battery to Watts in response to his request.

While these events were taking place on my front and engaging my attention, I received the message from G.H.Q. briefly telling me that as Marshal Foch would be coming to see me during the afternoon, I was to wait in for him. By this time my Head-quarters had been moved back to a little château in Dury, south of Amiens, as Villers-Bretonneux was required for Watts's Head-quarters, and it was here that I had my interview with Foch.

He arrived accompanied by General Weygand, and I received him in a frank and friendly manner.

To understand my position during this interview, several points must be borne in mind.

I was entirely ignorant of the Doullens Conference, and of the atmosphere approaching almost to panic which existed there, and of the absurd stories about the Fifth Army which were circulated in that assembly. I was equally unaware of the decisions arrived at. My own view of the situation generally was one of confidence and I was well satisfied with what the Fifth Army had done, and indeed I was proud of its conduct. I was under the illusion that the same view was held at G.H.Q. It should have been as well known there as it was at my own Head-quarters that the Army had been set the definite task of fighting a rear-guard action and of holding up the German attack with little or no support, in order to enable the Supreme Command to discover where the blow was really coming, to permit of Haig maintaining a firm hold of the Channel Ports, and to create the opportunity for a decisive blow against the Germans when the right time and place were decided on. I already could feel the weakening of the German attack and I realized that their great effort to break through was nearly foiled. I felt that the Army had faithfully carried out the terrible and heavy task that Haig had set it.

Moreover, I had always been particular during the four years of the War to maintain a friendly attitude towards French officers. We were always obliged to speak French ; I never spoke in my own tongue to a French General throughout the War. My French was quite good, though of the polite order more suitable to drawing-rooms than to a sharp argument : perhaps I had not a sufficient command of stern phrases, which were apparently required in such an interview as I had with Foch. All these facts placed me at a distinct disadvantage and exposed me to considerable surprise. Foch was peremptory, rude, and excited in his manner. He began at once by asking " Why I was at my Head-quarters and not with my troops in the fighting-line ? " He then said, " Why could I not fight as we had fought in the First Battle of Ypres in 1914 ? " " Why did the Army retire ? "

" What were my orders to the Army ? " He waited for no replies to any of these questions, and he did not expect one, except possibly the last. This was just as well, for any explanations would have probably led to an altercation. But the answers were indeed simple. I was at my Head-quarters because I had been ordered to meet him there, and also because it was my proper post. My task was not to lead a battalion or a company but to attend to what was going on along my extended front.

We were not holding the ground as we did in 1914, because, heavy though the odds against us had been in those weeks, they were more than doubled now. In the First Battle of Ypres, the Germans had not the massed superiority to maintain a continuous battle and they made a succession of attacks, with sometimes more than a day between each, enabling the defence to make a re-shuffle of its troops and give them some rest. In March, 1918, the German numbers were such that the attack was continuous for days and nights, and our outnumbered men never rested ; they fought, they marched, they dug, for days and nights together.

The Fifth Army had fought a rear-guard action because both strategical and tactical situations demanded such a course, it was " in accordance with plan "—in fact, with the plan of the Commander-in-Chief.

It can be imagined how surprised I was at this outburst on Foch's part. Surprise rather than indignation was my first impression. I now ask myself, how was it that a British General was placed in such a position ? How could it arise that he was exposed to such rudeness from an Allied officer ? How could Foch be so amazingly ignorant of the situation as not to realize the

splendid fight that the Fifth Army had put up?
How did he know so little that he could thus talk
to me, its Commander, of its deeds, when his own
French troops, fresh and in double or even
treble the numbers per yard of front, were falling
back faster than the tired Fifth Army, without
counter-attacks, often without even maintaining
a firm hold of their own front, and when our
own Third Army had already retired, thus exposing the left of the Fifth Army for three days?
When the Germans, having driven a hole into
the Third Army's front, were actually nearer
Amiens there than at any part of the front of the
Fifth Army?

How was it that he was so unaware of the real
facts? I was taken aback. But it can be asked,
was Foch's behaviour due entirely to his natural
and normal manners? He had come from
Doullens and from G.H.Q., where he had been
talking to British Ministers, British Generals and
Staff Officers. There can be little doubt that he
derived his impressions largely from what he had
heard there.

I kept my temper and told Foch what my orders
to the Army had been—namely, to fight a rear-
guard action, and thus gain time for the Allies
to send up their reserves. He did not inquire
into the position of the divisions of the Fifth
Army, nor their strength or condition, but said
in a loud, excited manner, " There must be no
more retreat, the line must now be held at all

costs," and then walked out of the room back to his car. He apparently did not know when supports could be expected and gave me no information on this important point or any other instructions or suggestions.

Even if my personal feelings are put aside, it is unfortunate from all points of view when those in positions of responsibility are exposed to such treatment at the hands of other Nationals, for it reacts over a wide field, and its repercussions extend in ever-widening circles. I cannot think that in the settlement of the peace of Europe or in the Councils of the Nations in the ensuing years the voice of the British Empire was accorded the weight and respect which was due to its power and its conduct in the War, and the seeds of this regrettable state of affairs can well have been sown at this interview, to grow later on into a formidable plant.

These orders of Foch, given without full knowledge of the facts, and without much serious consideration, could not be carried out, though I passed them on to my troops in accordance with military discipline. The French were yet to fall back another ten to twelve miles, and to lose Montdidier and Moreuil before the battle closed, while what was left of the Fifth Army only retired a further five or six miles, and that principally in order to bring it on to the same alignment as the Third Army on its left, though not a single fresh division was sent to its support.

The impression that Foch made on me was naturally not a favourable one. Excitable and evidently apt to jump to conclusions, he did not inspire me with respect or confidence.

Undoubtedly some authority was called for at this moment to co-ordinate the operations of the French and British Armies and to prevent Pétain from falling back on Paris in total disregard of his Allies. It is also true that even in this moment of crisis, even in the " *crise de nerfs* " from which the French were suffering, it is unlikely that they would ever have consented to a British generalissimo : the legend of the superiority of French leadership was naturally firmly established in France, and it found supporters even in England. Nevertheless, considering the question from a purely military standpoint as it appeared even *at that time*, could Foch's record as a commander be compared with Haig's ?

If we go into these questions we find that Foch had suffered a continuous series of reverses. Military critics among his own countrymen have pointed out that his leadership at Morhange was very faulty, and was largely responsible for the heavy defeat the French suffered there, and his conduct on the Marne in 1914 had nearly lost the War.[1] His operations in Artois in 1915 had

---

[1] See the reviews of the books by Colonel Mayer, by Colonel Lestern on the Marne, " The Battle of Morhange " by an anonymous writer, and Foch's own Memoirs, in *The Army Quarterly* of October 1930, July 1929, July 1931.

been costly failures. He had been removed from command after the Somme by his own Government ; for more than a year he had not been actively employed, and had been merely criticizing and advising.

Haig's record was very different. He had made mistakes, as every commander always has and always will. He had at times misjudged situations and men : nevertheless, from the very outset of the War he had continuously and steadfastly borne the burden of heavy responsibilities. Since his appointment as Commander-in-Chief he had shaken the German Army to its foundations on the Somme, had loyally supported Nivelle's offensive by the operations at Arras, and by his operations at Passchendaele and elsewhere in 1917 he had secured the French Army against perhaps an overwhelming disaster ! Furthermore, even this story, necessarily limited in its outlook, has shown that of the two Haig was far more international in his point of view. Foch was essentially a French General : on the other hand—and this cannot be too often emphasized—Haig's conceptions always embraced the situation of our Allies and contemplated the vast theatre of the whole War. He had fought the battles of 1915, 1916, and still more those of 1917, not necessarily that the British Army should win victories, but in order to help our Allies to win them or—equally important—to save our Allies from losing them ! Many of them were fought (notably the Battle of Loos) because they were strongly urged by Foch, against Haig's better judgment and contrary to his expressed opinion.

In 1918 Haig was the first among the Allied Commanders to see the significance in the change in the German resistance ; early in September he had informed his Government that " the character of the contest had changed, and that a decision in 1918 might be looked for." *At this time Foch was still preparing and basing his hopes on a campaign for* 1919 !

The final victories of August-October 1918, the foundations of which were " well and truly laid " by the Fifth Army in March, are among the greatest that any army or any General has ever won, and they were won by a British General and British soldiers, without the guidance of Foch, and sometimes in spite of his wishes.

But with the inveterate tendency of the British to belittle themselves and their own achievements, Haig has never been awarded by his own countrymen the position in their estimation which is justly his due. Let History say which of the two was the finer commander.

.   .   .   .   .   .

On the evening of this Tuesday I spoke on the telephone to the Chief of the General Staff and told him that the energy of the attacks was evidently weakening, and that the Germans were becoming worn out and very tired. Whenever

158

our men advanced to a counter-attack, unless the German machine guns could stop them, the enemy fell back. I went on to say that if G.H.Q. could send me two or three fresh divisions I could push the Germans in front of us back as far as the Somme. Lawrence laughed and said it was good to hear that we had plenty of fight still left, though no reinforcements at the moment could be sent.

VII [1]

Signs of weariness were now appearing in the enemy's ranks, and the Fifth Army, with the exhausted remnants of its divisions, their left on the Somme, still held fifteen miles of the front. The crossings over the river as far westwards as the Third Army's line, a distance of five miles, were only very weakly held by the hastily organized detachments which I had been able to send to Watts during the previous night.

Wednesday, March 27.

But the task of the Fifth Army was not yet completed and the remnants of its gallant soldiers had still grimly to keep going for several more days.

During this day Pellé's Corps on the right, with four divisions in line, held its front of eight miles firmly. Our cavalry and infantry of the III Corps, still with the French, played little or no part in this day's fighting. I was most anxious to get these divisions back under my orders, in

French V Corps.

[1] See Sketch Map 5, facing p. 168.

order to reinforce the unfortunate XIX Corps, which was very exhausted, and I was pressing the French for their return ; in consequence I ordered Butler, early in the morning, to get the 2nd Cavalry Division and Canadian Cavalry Brigade together and send them back to me, for I felt that a strong force of mobile cavalry was now badly wanted. The 14th Division also moved south-westwards to refit. A great deal of the III Corps artillery, however, was still kept with the French and fought for them all this day, as well as the whole of the artillery of the 36th Division and six batteries of 6″ howitzers of the XVIII Corps.

French II Cav. Corps.

Robillot's Corps on Pellé's left was driven back southwards, and a very considerable gap was thus created between it and the troops on its left— the French First Army under General Debeney, which was now beginning to arrive. If the fatal policy of falling back southwards to cover Paris had been persisted in, it would have precipitated dangerous crises for the Allies. But Foch's influence here was usefully exerted, and Pétain from now on did his best to maintain a united front.

French XXXV Corps.

During the afternoon and early the following morning the French XXXV Corps began to arrive, and came under Robillot's orders. It at first prolonged his left westwards to the south of Montdidier, but it left that town and a gap of six miles undefended on the right of the French VI Corps which belonged to Debeney's First Army.

French VI Corps.

160

This latter was also driven back during the 27th about nine miles, retiring westwards, and though it endeavoured to keep touch with the British, the direction of its retirement accentuated the six-mile gap between the two French Armies. During the following morning the remainder of the XXXV Corps came up, however, and filled this gap before anything disastrous had occurred.

The Germans walked into Montdidier (twenty-four miles S.E. of Amiens) unopposed about 7.30 this evening.

Meanwhile the French First Army was bringing up another Group, consisting of the 133rd and the 4th Cavalry Divisions, which was under the orders of General Mesple. He was to relieve our XVIII Corps, and take over its front. *Mesple's Group.*

Wednesday, the 27th, was another difficult day for the XVIII Corps, as the French still kept most of its guns, and the tired men again fought with insufficient artillery support. *XVIII Corps.*

To make matters worse, the Germans were able to exploit the gap which had been made on the front of the 36th Division on the previous evening, and the two brigades on the right only got back with great difficulty : two battalions of the Irish Fusiliers, finding themselves surrounded, resisted and held up the Germans for four hours before the survivors surrendered. By nightfall the division had fallen back about four miles, when it was at last relieved by the French 56th Division of Mesple's Group.

The German attack on the rest of the front of the XVIII Corps, and on the right of the XIX Corps, began about 10 a.m. The 30th Division held the front between the two villages of Bouchoir and Rouvroy, while the 20th Division was in close support. By 11 a.m. the enemy captured Bouchoir and Rouvroy, and our front here began to fall back, but a counter-attack by one battalion (12th King's) from the 20th Division drove back the Germans and a line was taken up which was held for the rest of the day, being relieved by the French early next morning. During the night Mesple's Group managed to relieve some of the right of the XVIII Corps, but the division on the left was not relieved till Thursday morning.

The 61st Division had been in reserve during the day, and I seized on it in the evening to assist the XIX Corps, for a new and alarming danger had suddenly burst upon the latter.

XIX
Corps.
The fact that the Third Army was several miles behind the left of the XIX Corps, for the third day in succession, provided the Germans with the opportunity of crossing the Somme, and during this day they took advantage of it, thus seriously threatening to cut off the Corps, as will shortly be related.

The chief cause for anxiety on the XIX Corps front during the day resulted from the developments of this situation, and an afternoon and night of agonizing anxiety was spent by the troops and their commanders in consequence, before the position could be made safe once more. But it is necessary to explain what took place during the day. On the right of the Corps the Germans began their attack between 7 and 8 a.m. The 24th and 8th Divisions, after heavy fighting and many small counter-attacks, maintained their positions with very little change. Rouvroy was lost by 11 a.m., but three companies led by Brig.-General R. W. Morgan retook it by midday.

But when the XVIII Corps fell back on the right, the Germans once again captured Rouvroy, and the 24th Division retired about a mile to keep in line with the XVIII Corps. Here it held the enemy for the rest of the day and prevented them from debouching out of the village. The 8th Division, displaying great steadiness and making energetic counter-attacks, also maintained its front intact throughout the day.

Much heavy fighting occurred along the rest of the Corps line, the enemy pressing vigorously, but immediate counter-attacks, organized with wonderful determination and energy by the Divisional and Brigade Commanders, stopped the German advances and in places threw them back.

On the left front the village of Proyart was held, and though its defenders repulsed one attack, it was eventually turned from the north, and fell into German hands about 10 a.m. Between the village and the river, a distance of about one and a half miles, the German 4th Guard Division was repulsed, with the aid of our aeroplanes, who swooped down on the attacking lines and " shot them up," a fine example of the close co-operation of all arms, by land and air, though by no means an uncommon one, for ever since the Battle of Passchendaele both the Germans and ourselves frequently made use of the Air Service in this manner.

The capture of Proyart exposed the left of the 39th Division, which was holding the line to the south of that village, and by noon the whole of this division had fallen back about two miles. This obliged the 66th Division also to retire a short distance, but it maintained this new line all day.

Meanwhile Watts had ordered a counter-attack to recapture Proyart. Three battalions, from the 8th and 50th Divisions, undertook this task— scarcely 300 weary men, infantry, pioneers and engineers. As they topped a rise about 3.30 p.m. they suffered considerable casualties from machine guns, but on they went. The Germans were in some old trenches and houses, and thick belts of old wire crossed their front, but the attackers found gaps and still advanced. After hard fighting they drove the Germans out of their position, capturing many prisoners. Here the line was established and held against hostile counter-attacks till the withdrawal next morning.

Further south, another magnificent example of British tenacity, energy and courage was displayed. Owing to a misunderstanding, three battalions of Riddell's Brigade, 50th Division, began to retire about 1 p.m., and the Germans quickly followed, pouring into the gap.

Riddell with his Brigade Staff, clerks, signallers, servants, all turned out and stopped the retreat in front of Harbonnières. He organized three battalions for an immediate counter-attack. On his left, all Malcolm's reserves of the 66th Division co-operated and advanced. On his right, two battalions under a Brigadier of 8th Division threw themselves into the struggle. At 3 p.m. all these different bodies, with the Staffs of the three brigades concerned, advanced to the counter-attack. They came over a rise and met, at a distance of 300 yards, eight or ten waves of advancing Germans. Our line threw itself down and opened a heavy fire on the leading waves of the enemy. Our guns caught the rear waves and punished them heavily. The Germans fell back. Our line swept on, capturing prisoners and machine guns, and on the whole front the line of the 50th Division was re-established.

But the defenders of the village of Vauvillers were running short of ammunition, and though it was being brought up, it could not reach them in time, and by 5 p.m. the Germans drove our men out of the village. They now enfiladed the left of the successful troops of the 50th Division and by evening these had to retire, but our line after a day of steady defence and most gallant counter-attacks was back not more than two miles.

It is now necessary to relate how the very dangerous threat emanating from the north of the Somme developed and forced the retirement of the whole of the XIX Corps.

By the early afternoon two brigades of the 16th Division, which were holding the line between Proyart and the Somme and which so far had repulsed all attacks on their front, found both their flanks turned and decided on a retirement behind Morcourt, a distance of under three miles. The orders did not reach three battalions, and these (a total of something more than 200) hung on till nightfall and then retired through the Germans to our lines, a very notable and gallant performance.

As the rest of the two brigades were taking up their new position west of Morcourt, to their surprise they came under heavy machine-gun fire from Cerizy. It was now evident that the Germans had crossed the river, and the two brigades fell back southwards to Lamotte, on the main Amiens road, and then rejoined Carey's Force, which was in position behind that village.

The presence of the Germans south of the river must now be accounted for. They had advanced against the Third Army the six or seven miles along the north bank of the Somme which lay beyond the left of the Fifth Army without much difficulty, but when they ran up against our 1st

Cavalry Division, which was now holding a line in advance of the right of the Third Army, they were held up by a stout defence. By way of turning it, they attempted to cross at Cerizy. The bridge here had been destroyed by the XIX Corps and the passage was obstinately defended by a company of 80 men of the 16th Division, which was all that the Fifth Army could spare to cover this exposed flank; the Germans, however, constructed a foot-bridge, and before midday they had forced the crossing. The only troops available to deal with this danger were two companies of Army Troop engineers, who had received no training as soldiers and could hardly handle a rifle. This attempt therefore failed to stop the Germans. Some engineers of the 16th Division were still near Morcourt, and they now faced north-west with their backs almost to the direction of the main German advance, and fired into the Germans advancing south from Cerizy. This delayed the enemy a short time.

Meanwhile General Feetham, 39th Division, had realized the danger, and collecting about 400 men of his own and of the 16th Divisions, attacked northwards towards Cerizy, and about 5 p.m. successfully seized a wood less than a mile south-west of the village.

The Germans were now reinforced and had four battalions across the river. They renewed their attack and drove our detachments back. A German battalion occupied Lamotte on the main road by 7 p.m. and during the night ambushed several parties of our men, who had as yet no idea of what had occurred.

Information had been sent to the Third Army that the enemy was crossing the Somme at Cerizy, thus creating a desperate situation for our troops still fighting several miles east of that place, and by orders from that Army the 1st Cavalry Division was withdrawn from its front and sent back to me. It crossed the river during the night and came into position mixed up with Carey's Force, between the Amiens high road and the Somme.

While these serious events were taking place on my left, I had gone out to see Maxse. I also visited Mesple at his Head-quarters. Nothing was organized there, and his Staff scarcely had a map of their front between them. Mesple did not appear to be a very intelligent or resolute-looking person, and I did not feel much confidence that the German attack would now be held. I looked in also on General Daly, commanding the 24th Division, and was back at my Head-quarters about 5 p.m. Here I found General Ruggles-Brise, Haig's Military Secretary, and not having an idea what he had come about, I sat him down to some tea. He then asked to see me alone and told me as nicely as he could that the Chief thought that I and my Staff must be very tired, so he had decided to put in Rawlinson and the Staff of the Fourth Army to take command. I was very surprised, and I suppose

MARCH 26TH 27TH 28TH 1918. SKETCH MAP 5.

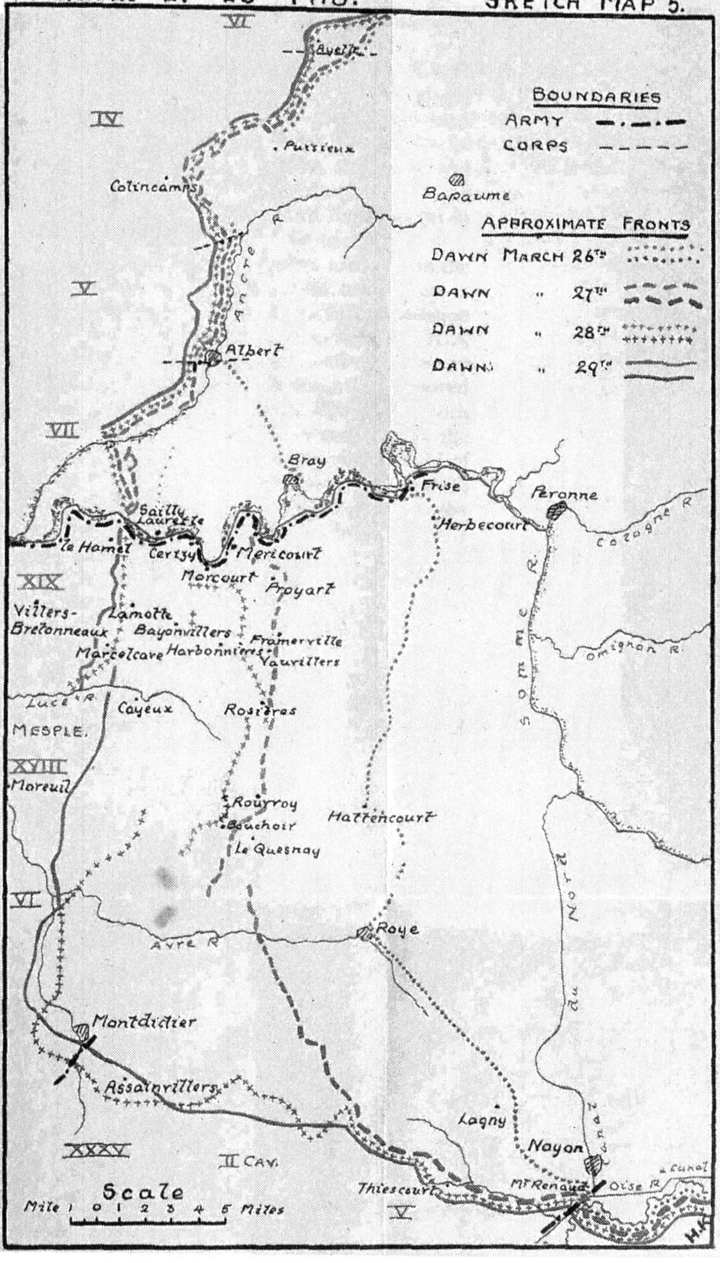

ed.

the Third A
mine at Ca
s for our tro
this place,
cavalry Divi
d back to
ays, but c
courts
the Sena
& p

s d

I was very hurt, but beyond saying " All right," I only asked when Rawlinson would be coming to take over.

I had not much leisure, however, to think over my own affairs, for the reports of the serious developments on the left of the XIX Corps were then coming in and steps to meet them had to be thought out and taken without delay. It was after this that we issued the orders for the move of the 61st Division by bus, and began to get in touch with the 1st Cavalry Division.

The 61st was the only division available in the XVIII Corps, and this was now ordered up as rapidly as possible in order to rectify this situation and to remove the danger threatening the XIX Corps. The Army Staff got hold of as many " buses " as possible and the division was moved during the night of the 27/28 to Marcelcave, with the object of making a counter-attack from the south against Lamotte and then, with the aid of the 1st Cavalry Division, which was to co-operate on its left, to drive the Germans back across the Somme, thus freeing the XIX Corps from the grave menace which threatened it.

The day was by no means over, and in fact most of our days in the Fifth Army during this critical battle were of 24 hours : there were no " 8-hour days " for any of us !

Before relating how the XIX Corps extricated itself from its dangerous position, the astonishing adventures of the three Irish battalions of

169   M

the 16th Division already referred to must be described. These battalions held their positions of the morning, nearly two miles east of Mericourt, all day and repulsed all attacks. They realized that they were isolated, but decided to wait till dark before attempting to get away. After dark they marched in column down the road to the bridge over the Somme north of Mericourt. This was strongly held by the Germans. They then marched down the tow-path to Cerizy, but took the wise precaution of sending forward a reconnoitring patrol. This found a German picquet on the bridge, which the main body surprised and shot, and then rushed the bridge. They were now truly in the enemy's country, on the north bank. However, no one expected them, and they again stuck to the tow-path on the far bank, and reached the next bridge at Sailly Laurette without incident. Here they rushed another German picquet, recrossed the river and marched into our own lines near Hamel. A truly wonderful example of courage and initiative.

The situation of the XIX Corps that night was as follows : the divisions had fought splendidly and shown a wonderful spirit after the week of storm and stress to which they had been exposed. There was no doubt that the vim of the German attack was disappearing. Comparatively little ground had been lost along the front, but behind the left flank the Germans were on the south bank of the Somme at Cerizy, in Lamotte on the main road, as well as close to the river near Morcourt. The 39th Division was already facing east, north and west. About 11 p.m. a line facing west astride the main road was formed by two companies of engineers.

The three Brigadiers were completely cut off from their Divisional Head-quarters, and they very wisely decided to withdraw south and take up a new line Harbonnières–Bayonvillers, at 2 a.m. Two officers took a message, and by stalking got round Lamotte and delivered it. Then the Brigadiers received a message from their division, instructing them to hold on, as a counter-attack by the 61st Division on Lamotte was being organized; but by 4 a.m. the division had received orders sanctioning a withdrawal, and it was able to pass these on to its Brigadiers.

While the Brigadiers of the 39th Division had been anxiously discussing their situation, the Commanders of the three divisions—the 8th, 50th and 66th—were also holding a council at Cayeux. The danger of all three divisions being cut off completely if they remained in their present positions was obvious, and at 1 a.m. they communicated with their Corps.

This situation had already been referred to me, but I had been ordered by Foch to hold our ground at all costs until relieved by the French, and I was still anxious to comply with these orders if there was any prospect of French relief being in sight. But it was now evident that if we held on, the Corps would be destroyed. My Staff got through to Foch and he was roused from his bed, and after the situation had been clearly put to him he consented to the orders for a retirement being issued.

Such questions as this should have been referred to British G.H.Q. Haig was still responsible for the security of British troops, and I cannot say that I approved of the Fifth Army being handed over body and soul to the French even if Foch was Generalissimo.[1]

There can be no question that Foch's orders to me nearly brought about the destruction of the XIX Corps, and did in fact cost the lives of many British soldiers. If the order to retire could have been issued in time to enable the divisions to withdraw the previous night, they could have retired from their dangerous positions and taken up the new line before daybreak on the 28th with little loss, and with much better prospects of holding it. Foch knew, or ought to have known, that my troops were extremely exhausted after a

[1] After I had handed over to Rawlinson, G.H.Q. wrote him a letter directing him to remember that his responsibilities were first for the safety of the British forces under his command. Such orders should have been issued to me also, with a copy to the French, immediately on my being placed under the orders of Fayolle on the 25th of March. It would have strengthened my hand considerably at this crisis, and would have been a support which was but due to me.

week of desperate fighting, that their left flank was very exposed to attack for five miles, and that no reliefs were coming up for several days yet. Perhaps he was in the habit of issuing such orders to his French Generals, who evidently did not take them too literally, for the French troops on my right continued to make considerable retirements during the 27th. It is easy to say that a position must be held " at all costs," and there are times when it should be held to the last, but when such an order is given without due regard to the circumstances it is a grave error and can be the cause of disastrous consequences. That Foch's hasty and ill-considered order did not lead to a disaster was only due to the gallantry of the exhausted fragments of the British divisions and the steady tactical leadership of their officers.

VIII [1]

The last day of my career as a soldier opened, therefore, with renewed anxieties and further calls for decisions.

The problem was how to withdraw the XIX Corps from the very critical position in which it had been placed through no fault of its own, and to supervise the carrying out of this difficult operation.

But before dealing with this, let me briefly relate the events of the previous day along the

[1] See Sketch Map 5, facing p. 168.

original Army front. On our right, Humbert's Third Army had steadied, and held its line more or less firmly against the attack of the tired German divisions. In fact, Humbert, with a sound military instinct, had ordered an advance against what was now the flank of a great German salient. In one place some ground was gained and the village of Assainvillers retaken, but on the whole little change took place. The French had not got the power in them to drive a large hole into the side of the German attack. The right of the French First Army lost ground south and north of Montdidier, but on fresh reinforcements coming up, some of this ground was recaptured and the German advance stayed. Mesple's Group and the French VI Corps, however, did not do well, and this unfortunately put an additional burden on the remnants of our divisions of the XVIII and XIX Corps, the latter being already in a most dangerous situation owing to the inrush of Germans behind its left.

The position of the Corps in a pronounced salient, with the French VI Corps on the right and our Third Army on the left both far behind it, made a retirement in any case inevitable, but now that the enemy was established in Lamotte and Cerizy, behind its left and centre, the situation was urgent and critical.

Similar situations had been met before by the commanders in the Fifth Army during the course of the battle, though not in so pronounced a degree, but we had withdrawn in time and extricated many units from dangerous positions, while keeping the line intact. We could have done the same in this case also if we had been left to our own initiative and military knowledge, alarming as was the situation, without the heavy losses which compliance with the order of Foch entailed.

Watts recognized the situation here as quickly as I did, but out of a misplaced desire to be loyal to Foch and our Allies, and having received no qualifying instruction or support from G.H.Q., I hesitated to ignore Foch's order to hold on at all costs.

I was to blame, and I should undoubtedly have acted entirely on my own judgment and ignored these orders. Three times during the course of the battle I received similar orders from my superior—" the position was to be held at all costs." The first occasion was to hold the Péronne bridge-head east of the Somme. I did not act on this order, and retired across the Somme as soon as my front was broken in two places on the 22nd—at Caulaincourt and Nobescourt Farm.

Some critics may say that I was wrong in departing from my orders, but the situation was desperate and in my judgment no other course was open to me. The responsibility was certainly great, but even now as I try to reconstruct the past in the peace and quiet of my study it is my firm conviction that if we had not retired when we did, our troops east of the river would never have got back at all !

It has also been suggested that, if I had held the Péronne bridge-head, I could have re-formed and reorganized behind the river the divisions which had been so battered in the previous fighting. The futility of the suggestion will be at once apparent to the readers of this chapter. There was no question of re-forming the divisions which had suffered most in the early fighting, for there were no adequate supports to take their place or to cover them. They had to carry on the fighting themselves, and in fact did so for five more days ; and by getting across the river when they did, the divisions of the XIX Corps were able to organize an adequate defence, which would certainly not have been the case if they had been driven back in confusion with the enemy close on their heels. As a matter of fact, these divisions held the river line for two days, with the Armies to the north and south falling back several miles on both flanks. Watts's judgment and my decision were right, and it was fortunate that we acted accordingly ; our action saved the Fifth Army and the British cause from defeat and ruin. Criticisms of the retirement across the Somme do not take into consideration the further disasters which would have overtaken the Fifth Army if it had attempted to continue holding the Péronne bridge-head when the Third Army retired on its left, which it did the next day.

The occupation of Lamotte by the enemy on March 28 provides a striking illustration of the position in which the Army might have found itself!

The second occasion on which I received orders from the Supreme Command was once again to hold the line of the Somme "at all costs." On this occasion I did keep the Fifth Army on that line for two days while our neighbours fell back, and the price was the annihilation of the devoted South African Brigade and several other determined and courageous detachments. It would, in fact, have been better to have retired twenty-four hours earlier, and kept more in line with the Armies on my right and left.

Foch's order was the third one of this nature I had received, and though I now blame myself for not acting on my own better judgment, the Fifth Army at least did its duty in accordance with the very best traditions of the British people, and it is the last Army of whom it can be said that it retired too soon, or that its retirement was the reason for the retreat of others. The facts are exactly the contrary.

But to return to the 28th of March. Orders were issued about 5 o'clock in the morning for a new line to be taken up, leaving the 24th Division still holding its line west of Rouvroy like a condemning finger pointing into the face of the

Thursday, March 28.

177

Germans, while the three divisions were to take up a line now facing north-east and south of Lamotte. Actually, this plan was subsequently modified, and the 24th Division was brought back in line with the rest of the Army and the French. The retirement of the divisions of the XIX Corps had to be carried out by daylight, with the enemy pressing round both flanks, and treading closely on their heels. Gaps inevitably occurred, new lines were soon enfiladed, and the exhausted men only got back with difficulty, at the cost of many more casualties, and exposed to moments of sudden and great anxiety. The energy, devotion and resolution of their commanders and officers, coupled with the steadfastness of the men, saved them and enabled the Corps to fall back some six miles and eventually take up a line with the French on the right and Carey's Force on the left on a position behind Marcelcave to the Somme.

The 61st Division attacked Lamotte about noon, after a night in the buses, but being enfiladed by machine guns, failed to retake the village. Riddell, with the 50th Division, and its commander, Jackson, again on this day saved the situation by their prompt decision, Jackson sounding a hunting-horn to encourage his men to get forward ! How he came to have a hunting-horn on him I could never guess, but I dare say its notes, so familiar to English ears, were encouraging to our tired men.

The XVIII Corps, having held the front line during the early part of the day, was eventually relieved by the French, and its divisions withdrawn to rest and refit, but I sent the 20th Division, now reduced to about 1000 men, across to help Watts, and called up the 18th Division and the 2nd Cavalry Division from our III Corps with Humbert's Third Army to support our weary and shaken line. These were the last operations I was ever to direct as a soldier.

XVIII Corps.

At 4.30 that afternoon, Rawlinson arrived to take over the command. I told him all I could of our situation, and as I felt that I should only be an embarrassment to him in exercising his new command, I left Dury, not at all sure where I was to get a bed or dinner that night.

Before I handed over the command, the task of the Fifth Army can be said to have been completed. Very little more ground was lost, and that principally by the French. Within a few days the remnants of my exhausted divisions had been relieved by fresh troops, after having performed feats of gallantry and endurance that will be a military byword for many years to come.

A retreat is not necessarily a defeat. Some of the greatest victories in military history have been based on retreats. The retreat to Moscow and the consequent destruction of Napoleon's army is one example. Wellington conducted many retreats which led to great victories during the

Peninsular War—the retreat to the lines of Torres Vedras—the retreat before Salamanca—the retreat from Burgos : these do not complete the list. The retreat from the battlefields of Ligny and Quatre Bras led to the victory of Waterloo.

If the Fifth Army had attempted to hold their ground at all costs—if the tactics had not been those of a great rear-guard action—the whole Army might have been overwhelmed, in fact almost certainly would have been, in the first two or three days' fighting. There would then have been a gap, not of two or three miles which could be filled somehow—but of forty miles ! It does not require a great stretch of imagination to see the disastrous consequences to the Allies if such a position had been created.

The fighting retreat of the Fifth Army was no new operation of war, though perhaps conducted on a greater scale and under conditions of more difficulty and stress than any previous example. Its material effects were vital to the Allied cause. The highest hopes of the Germans, naturally so encouraged by the collapse of Russia, had been staked on this gigantic onslaught. And now the great effort of the German High Command to defeat the British, to cut them off from the French, and to drive them into the sea, had been defeated. The German Army was stopped, it had shot its bolt ; the high hopes of a great, decisive, and above all a *final* victory, were dead.

From now on, though it still put forth at times a last despairing display of its ancient fierce strength, like the last flickerings of a dying candle, its moral rapidly sank. ,

The Channel Ports were secure, and though the few divisions of the Fifth Army were shattered and almost destroyed, Haig had economized his forces, and still had many divisions in hand for the great counter-strokes, when in four months' time the British Army was able to advance on broad fronts, gaining greater victories (if victories and defeats can be measured by captured prisoners and trophies) than it has ever done in its previous history.

Of the results of this battle the Germans themselves have written :

> When a great attack, from which something decisive is expected, fails hopelessly with heavy losses, the cohesion of an army is more shaken than by an unsuccessful defensive battle.

A French officer wrote :

> The moral of the German attacking divisions was very good. They were cheered by their successes at Riga and Caporetto, buoyed up by hope of victory at a single blow, an end to all their miseries. But if an instant success was not attained, their moral, thus disillusioned, would fall.

As indeed it did !

On March 27, General Malcolm, commanding

the 66th Division, which had just carried out a successful counter-attack and driven back the Germans, making some prisoners, while walking back to his Head-quarters met a French officer, who in very evident anxiety inquired of the situation. Malcolm replied : " It is quite good ; we have won the War."

He realized the failing energy, the growing weariness of the German troops in his front ; he could feel the attack was stayed—the situation saved.

Lord Birkenhead, in his book, " Turning Points of History," writing of the triumph of the Fifth Army in this battle, says :

> On them fell the brunt of the attack. The Armies on his flanks did not hold as firm as they might have done. Gough had neither adequate rear lines of defence nor reserves. Yet with such tenacity and courage did he continue to oppose and muffle the enemy's advance that, after the first terrible fortnight was passed, the front still stood, and Ludendorff's last throw had patently failed. Amiens was saved ; so was Paris ; so were the Channel Ports. So was France. So was England.

What was the state of these steadfast and heroic men to whom these great results were due ? The story, as I have briefly written it, tells something of the heavy casualties, of the dead lying thickly across every mile of the fiercely disputed battle-field, of the wounded and prisoners left behind in the hands of the enemy. Of the survivors, an average of little more than 1000 could still stand to arms in the divisions whose strength on paper should have stood at 10,000 infantry ! Some battalions were reduced to 50 men. The Staffs, the clerks, the engineers, had all given up their ordinary functions to shoulder a rifle.

The cavalry had played a great part in the battle. Their mobility, and their capacity to cross any country on horses and therefore to get rapidly from place to place, made them far more powerful than· their mere numbers would suggest. They were quickly able to cover an exposed flank, to seize a position or to threaten one. They were rushed from one position to another to fill a gap, and saved many a critical situation. They fought mounted or dismounted as opportunity offered. Their great value during these ten days should never be forgotten. Had the Germans been able to make use of cavalry of the same calibre during these events it is more than probable that the whole course of the battle would have been altered.

An instructive commentary on the value of cavalry in a crisis is supplied by the fact that, some time before the battle, several regiments of yeomanry had been dismounted and given bicycles. In the battle they abandoned their bicycles and were hastily remounted on any spare horses that could be collected, as the value of mounted troops was keenly realized.

The energy and the devoted courage of the gunners had saved many a situation, had covered and protected their comrades and had taken a heavy toll of the Germans, often exposed in thick lines across the open ground.

Our airmen had also largely abandoned their ordinary functions of observation to concentrate on close fighting, swooping on the enemy's infantry; everything had to give way to the imperious necessity of giving the closest support to the infantrymen.

The state of exhaustion to which these were reduced can be realized from their own diaries. One says:

> The troops were very badly in need of a rest; there was no such thing as a platoon or company, and the junior officers (mostly aged 19) were for the most part incapable of dealing with the situation. It appeared absolutely necessary that if the division was to be of any further use, it should be withdrawn from the line and given an opportunity to reorganize and pull itself together, even if only six hours could be allowed. This state of affairs was explained to the Corps, but the latter replied that such a course was unfortunately impossible and that the division must hold on in the line for the present.

This was a division which had been continuously in the line since the battle opened, and yet it lost little ground on the 27th—and counter-attacked the Germans with success.

Another diary says :

The troops were dazed and weakened by their long period of fighting without rest. There was no sign of panic, and any attempts to withdraw were quite orderly, and the men obeyed willingly when ordered to return to their position, but they appeared to have lost the sense of reasoning and it was difficult to make them understand.

Another diary says :

Men who are weary are unaccountable for their actions. They had fought for seven days and nights and could not have totalled eight hours' sleep in that time. They had dug trenches out of number, and had covered (at a low estimate) sixty miles, if one considers marches, counter-attacks, etc.

The Germans also were very exhausted. Our retirements were usually made at a slow walk, they following at a distance of a few hundred yards at the same pace, and halting when the British line halted and turned round.

IX

Little remains to be told. Within a week I was ordered home and placed on half-pay. Haig sent for me to tell me the Cabinet's decision. He told me that there was to be an inquiry and that my Corps Commanders would be called to give evidence. He also told me that the Prime

Minister had blamed me greatly, especially for not holding the line of the Somme.

How little did the Prime Minister know of the strategy that led up to the battle, and of the tactics which influenced its course, and even of the map ; for the Somme only covered eleven miles of a battle front which extended· over fifty-five miles when that of the Third Army is included ; and the Fifth Army maintained its hold on the line of that river for two days while the French on the right, and still more so the Third Army on the left, had fallen back many miles on its flanks.

I did not say much to Haig—I did not want to bother him. I simply said, " Never mind now, sir. I am not going to say anything : you have too many very serious matters to think about, and your responsibilities and burdens at the moment are much too heavy for me to add anything to them. Don't worry about me," and I left.

When I reached home I heard nothing whatever from the War Office, and so eventually I asked for an interview with the Secretary of State for War (Lord Derby), and I saw him on the 8th of April.

He was suave and pleasant in manner, but he did not enter into any details of the battle. He told me that an inquiry was going to be held into the circumstances of the battle, that my Corps Commanders and other witnesses would be called, and that if I were exonerated from blame, as he hoped and felt sure would be the case, I should be reinstated.

I heard no more, however, and after writing twice to inquire the date of the proposed inquiry, I received a letter from the War Office in which I was informed that no inquiry was to be held, and that I was mistaken in thinking that a promise to that effect had been made!

I also saw Lord Milner, a Member of the War Council. I found him polite, but quite unsympathetic. It was evident that he thought the Fifth Army was entirely responsible for the loss of ground, material, etc., in the battle. It was he who said to me, "You must admit, General Gough, that your troops sometimes left their positions before they should have done."

It is natural, and I hope pardonable, if feelings of indignation still rise within me at conclusions so hastily arrived at and so firmly held.

How many units had fought to the last, leaving their bodies to mark the spot of their gallant sacrifice?

The salient facts of the battle ought to have been known to Ministers by this time, and it seems curious that even the heroic conduct of the South Africans was unknown to Lord Milner.

I had hoped that the Fifth Army as a whole would be withdrawn to rest and refit under my orders after the stern trial through which it had just passed. It would have been a powerful and homogeneous body, animated and strengthened by the comradeship and confidence which is only born of duty faithfully achieved in days of a common adversity. We could then have returned again to the front to take an honourable part in those great victories, the foundations of which had been laid on the bodies of our dead and in the spent and exhausted souls of the survivors. But it was not to be, and I was not allowed to play any further part in the great events of the War which were yet to follow.

On the 9th April Mr. Lloyd George offered his explanation of recent events in France to his then faithful followers in the House of Commons, and made several direct statements which most ungenerously placed blame on the Fifth Army in general, as well as on myself in particular. These statements were quite inaccurate. He made several other more or less indirect statements, which in a thinly veiled way also implied blame on the Army, and made invidious and very misleading comparisons.

For example, he inferred that the Fifth Army was retreating precipitately while the Third Army held, "never giving way 100 yards to the attack of the enemy." Without in any way disparaging the Third Army, the readers of these pages will immediately recognize not only the incorrectness but also the absurdity of this statement. Mr. Lloyd George stated, in his now-famous story of Carey's Force, that " He (Brig.-General

Carey) gathered together signalmen, engineers, and Labour battalions, odds and ends of machine gunners, everybody he could find, and threw them into the line and held up the German Army and closed the gap on the way to Amiens for about six days." General Carey did nothing of the kind. He was not in the slightest degree responsible for the formation, organization or posting of this force. He was away on leave in England when it was formed and posted, and he did not take command of it until it had been in position for two days. This book clearly shows that such formations as these " forces " were envisaged and provided for weeks before the attack, and were part of our defensive scheme. This force, which was only one of several, organized by the Corps as well as by the Army, was entirely formed, organized and posted under my directions and by my Staff.

The retreat, in fact, was a clearly defined manœuvre foreseen months before it took place, sanctioned by the Commander-in-Chief, and planned and prepared in great detail. The impressions left by Mr. Lloyd George in this speech were almost uniformly false and misleading. The Fifth Army faithfully carried out the heavy task allotted to it. There was no disaster : there was no defeat.

The facts should have been known to the Prime Minister by that time, and there was little excuse in any circumstances for making these false

statements. Since then much has been cleared
up and the facts are now better known. Mr.
Lloyd George, however, has never taken any
steps to withdraw the undeserved and ungenerous
comments he made on those heroic men who
endured the main burden of that terrific ordeal
in March 1918, over-stretched and grossly undermanned as was their line, largely because of his
own policy and action (or rather his inaction !)
and of his faith in anyone rather than in his own
countrymen.

To this day the reverberations of his ill-considered speech are heard, and he has done nothing
to dispel the ignorant rumours which he initiated.
To the memory of those thousands of gallant
men who lie in that stricken area, men who
gave their lives for the cause he represented—to
their mothers and sisters who may still feel the
wounds caused by unfounded suggestions that
their loved ones were not heroes but cowards,
and to those who, by some more favourable
chance, survived the greatest battle in history,
some acknowledgment is owing. It is sometimes
said that their honour can now with confidence
be left to posterity. It is an easy attitude to
take up, but does it suffice ?

Suddenly deprived of a Staff, of all my records,
papers and means of communication with my
corps and divisions, I was never able to thank
the men of my Army officially for their faithful,
devoted courage, for all they had done, suffered

and achieved for their comrades, for Britain, and for the Empire. Some of the survivors I have been able to thank individually, others indirectly, but this book at last gives me an opportunity of telling all of them how sincerely, how deeply, I thank them. I hope its pages amply prove my appreciation of their splendid character and conduct. I know that, like every other general who has commanded troops in battle, I was guilty of mistakes and errors of judgment. " The man who has never made a mistake has never made war " is a saying attributed to Napoleon. But whatever may have been my shortcomings, I am deeply conscious that my Army never failed me.

I think it was said by the Greeks that " No man deserves to live who fears to die." Then indeed the officers and men of the Fifth Army deserve to live—at least in the memories of their countrymen—for they knew how, and were not afraid, to die.

In an appendix to this book will be found the Order of Battle of the Fifth Army on the morning of the 21st of March 1918—a list of the gallant units who took the first shock of the great assault. It will repay study. In that list will be found the names of famous regiments whose colours have waved over many a battlefield ; in their ranks, and those of the auxiliary services, were men from all parts of the Empire, called together by a stern sense of duty. No greater battle honours were ever won than in this eight-days' inferno, when battalions dwindled to platoons, and when companies fought till no man remained alive.

To those who survived I say : Hold up your heads high with pride. History will proclaim the greatness of what you did. It can be said of no other troops that they did more to win the War. You are the remnants of a gallant band of brothers buffeted by adversity and grievously maligned, yet your spirit is too fine to be damped by such misfortunes : you are the men on whom Britain is based.

To my countrymen from all parts of our wide Empire I say : Read, and think of what it meant to you, this band of men who stood unflinchingly between you and all that defeat meant. And realize that many thousands of the survivors live to-day, passing unnoticed in a civilian crowd ; you may meet them day by day, unhonoured and unknown. Acknowledge their valour as and when you can ; it is too easy to forget.

To the relatives of the dead I say : Your men died as heroes among heroes. They faced overwhelming odds with a courage beyond the power of words to praise. Battered and bruised, they hung on to the last to enable their comrades to retire, so as to continue the battle—and to save Britain. When the end came they had no regrets ; they had done their duty. There is a broad wreath of British dead in that desolate land, which has now become once again a smiling countryside. The rows of crosses mark for ever the scenes of their valiant deeds : history at least will give them the great honour they earned. Britain can ill spare such men : they are of the breed which has made her honoured and powerful throughout the world.

APPENDIX

APPENDIX

From the Right of the Line

III Corps

Lt.-General Sir R. H. K. Butler.
B.G.G.S.   Brig.-General C. G. Fuller.
D.A.Q.M.G. Brig.-General J. F. I. H. Doyle.
C.R.A.   Brig.-General T. A. Tancred.
C.H.A.   Brig.-General A. E. J. Perkins.
C.E.   Brig.-General A. Rolland.

58th (2/1st London) Division

Major-General A. B. E. Cator.
G.S.O. 1. Lt.-Colonel R. H. Mangles.

173rd Infantry Brigade.—Brig.-General R. B. Worgan.
   2/2nd London. 3rd London. 2/4th London.
174th Infantry Brigade.—Brig.-General C. G. Higgins.
   6th London. 7th London. 8th London.
175th Infantry Brigade.—Brig.-General H. C. Jackson.
   9th London. 2/10th London. 12th London.
Pioneers.—1/4th Suffolk.

18th Division

Major-General R. P. Lee.
G.S.O. 1. Lt.-Colonel W. D. Wright, V.C.

53rd Infantry Brigade.—Brig.-General H. W. Higginson.
    10th Essex. 8th R. Berks. 7th R. West Kent.
54th Infantry Brigade.—Brig.-General L. W. de V. Sadleir-Jackson.
    11th Roy. Fus. 7th Bedfordshire. 6th Northamptonshire.
55th Infantry Brigade.—Brig.-General E. A. Wood.
    7th Queen's. 7th Buffs. 8th East Surrey.
Pioneers.—8th R. Sussex.

14th Division

Major-General Sir Victor Couper.
G.S.O. 1. Lt.-Colonel A. C. Bayley.

41st Infantry Brigade.—Brig.-General P. C. B. Skinner.
    8th K.R.R.C. 7th Rifle Brigade. 8th Rifle Brigade.
42nd Infantry Brigade.—Brig.-General G. N. B. Forster.
    5th Oxford L.I. 9th K.R.R.C. 9th Rifle Brigade.
43rd Infantry Brigade.—Brig.-General R. S. Tempest.
    6th Somerset L.I. 9th Scottish Rifles. 7th K.R.R.C.
Pioneers.—11th King's Own.

APPENDIX

2nd *Cavalry Division*

Major-General W. H. Greenly.
G.S.O. 1. Lt.-Colonel H. de Burgh.

3rd Cavalry Brigade.—Brig.-General J. A. Bell-Smyth.
4th Hussars. 5th Lancers. 16th Lancers.
4th Cavalry Brigade.—Brig.-General T. T. Pitman.
6th Dragoon Guards. 3rd Hussars. Oxford-shire Hussars.
5th Cavalry Brigade.—Lt.-Colonel W. F. Collins.
Royal Scots Greys. 12th Lancers. 20th Hussars.

3rd *Cavalry Division*

Brig.-General A. E. W. Harman.
G.S.O. 1. Lt.-Colonel J. A. Muirhead.

6th Cavalry Brigade.—Brig.-General A. Seymour.
3rd Dragoon Guards. 1st Royal Dragoons. 10th Hussars.
7th Cavalry Brigade.—Brig.-General B. P. Portal.
7th Dragoon Guards. 6th Innis. Dragoons. 17th Lancers.
Canadian Cavalry Brigade.—Brig.-General Rt. Hon. J. E. B. Seely.
R. Canadian Dragoons. Lord Strathcona's Horse. Fort Garry Horse.

XVIII Corps

Lt.-General Sir Ivor Maxse.
B.G.G.S.   Brig.-General S. E. Holland.
D.A.Q.M.G. Brig.-General L. H. Abbott.
C.R.A.   Brig.-General D. J. M. Fasson.
C.H.A.   Brig.-General H. E. J. Brake.
C.E.   Brig.-General H. G. Joly de Lotbinière.

36th Division

Major-General O. S. W. Nugent.
G.S.O. 1. Lt.-Colonel C. O. Place.

107th *Infantry Brigade.*—Brig.-General W. M. Withycombe.
    2nd R. Irish Rifles. 1st R. Irish Rifles. 15th R. Irish Rifles.
108th *Infantry Brigade.*—Brig.-General C. R. J. Griffith.
    12th R. Irish Rifles. 1st R. Irish Fus. 9th R. Irish Fus.
109th *Infantry Brigade.*—Brig.-General W. F. Hessey.
    1st R. Innis. Fus. 9th R. Innis. Fus. 2nd R. Innis. Fus.
Pioneers.—16th R. Irish Rifles.

30th Division

Major-General W. de L. Williams.
G.S.O. 1. Lt.-Colonel H. R. Blore.

21st *Infantry Brigade.*—Brig.-General G. D. Goodman.
    2nd Wiltshire. 2nd Green Howards. 17th Manchester.

89th Infantry Brigade.—Brig.-General F. C. Stanley.
17th King's. 18th King's. 19th King's.
90th Infantry Brigade.—Lt.-Colonel H. S. Poyntz.
2nd Bedfordshire. 2nd Royal Scots Fus. 16th
Manchester.
Pioneers.—11th South Lancs.

61st Division

Major-General C. Mackenzie.
G.S.O. 1. Brig.-General R. O'H. Livesay.

182nd Infantry Brigade.—Brig.-General W. K. Evans.
2/6th R. Warwicks. 2/7th R. Warwicks.
2/8th Worcester.
183rd Infantry Brigade.—Brig.-General A. H. Spooner.
9th Royal Scots. 5th Gordon Highs. 8th A. &
S. Highs.
184th Infantry Brigade.—Brig.-General Hon. R. White.
2/5th Gloucester. 2/4th Oxford. 2/4th R.
Berks.
Pioneers.—1/5th D.C.L.I.

XIX Corps

Lt.-General Sir H. E. Watts.
B.G.G.S.   Brig.-General C. N. Macmullen.
D.A.Q.M.G. Brig.-General A. J. G. Moir.
C.R.A.   Brig.-General W. B. R. Sandys.
C.H.A.   Brig.-General C. G. Pritchard.
C.E.   Brig.-General A. G. Bremner.

24th Division

Major-General A. C. Daly.
G.S.O. 1. Lt.-Colonel J. H. Mackenzie.

17th *Infantry Brigade.*—Brig.-General P. V. P. Stone.
8th R. West Surrey. 1st Royal Fus. 3rd Rifle
Brigade.

72nd *Infantry Brigade.*—Brig.-General R. W. Morgan
(on leave 15th–24th March). *Acting-Brig.*—Colonel L. J. Wyatt.
9th East Surrey. 8th R. West Kent. 1st North
Staffs.

73rd *Infantry Brigade.*—Brig.-General W. J. Dugan.
9th R. Sussex. 7th Northampton. 13th Middlesex.

Pioneers.—12th Notts and Derby.

66th Division

Major-General Neill Malcolm.
G.S.O. 1. Lt.-Colonel A. R. Burrowes.

197th *Infantry Brigade.*—Brig.-General O. C. Borrett.
6th Lancs. Fus. 2/7th Lancs. Fus. 2/8th
Lancs. Fus.

198th *Infantry Brigade.*—Brig.-General A. J. Hunter.
4th East Lancs. 2/5th East Lancs. 9th Manchester.

199th *Infantry Brigade.*—Brig.-General G. C. Williams.
2/5th Manchester, 2/6th Manchester. 2/7th
Manchester.

Pioneers.—5th Border.

APPENDIX

VII Corps

Lt.-General Sir W. N. Congreve, V.C.

B.G.G.S.   Brig.-General Hon. A. G. A. Hore-
Ruthven, V.C.
D.A.Q.M.G. Brig.-General A. A. McHardy.
C.R.A.   Brig.-General K. K. Knapp.
C.H.A.   Brig.-General F. H. Metcalfe.
C.E.   Brig.-General R. D. Petrie.

1st Cavalry Division (in Reserve)

Major-General R. L. Mullens.
G.S.O. 1. Lt.-Colonel S. F. Muspratt.

1st Cavalry Brigade.—Brig.-General E. Makins.
2nd Dragoon Guards. 5th Dragoon Guards.
11th Hussars.
2nd Cavalry Brigade.—Brig.-General D. J. E. Beale-
Browne.
4th Dragoon Guards. 9th Lancers. 18th Hussars.
9th Cavalry Brigade.—Brig.-General D'A. Legard.
8th Hussars. 19th Hussars. 15th Hussars.

16th Division

Major-General Sir C. P. A. Hull.
G.S.O. 1. Lt.-Colonel L. C. Jackson.

47th Infantry Brigade.—Brig.-General H. G. Gregorie.
6th Connaught Rangers. 2nd Leinster. 1st R.
Munster Fus.

48th *Infantry Brigade.*—Brig.-General F. W. Ramsay.
    1st R. Dublin Fus.   2nd R. Dublin Fus.   2nd R.
    Munster Fus.
49th *Infantry Brigade.*—Brig.-General P. Leveson-
Gower.
    2nd R. Irish.   7th (South Irish Horse) R. Irish.
    7/8th R. Innis. Fus.
Pioneers.—11th Hampshire.

39th *Division* (in Reserve)

Major-General E. Feetham.
G.S.O. 1. Lt.-Colonel F. W. Gossett.

116th *Infantry Brigade.*—Brig.-General M. L. Hornby.
    11th R. Sussex.   13th R. Sussex.   1/1st Herts.
117th *Infantry Brigade.*—Brig.-General G. A. Army-
tage.
    16th Notts and Derby.   17th K.R.R.C.   16th
    Rifle Brigade.
118th *Infantry Brigade.*—Brig.-General E. H. C. P.
Bellingham.
    1/6th Cheshire.   4/5th Black Watch.   1/1st
    Cambridge.
Pioneers.—13th Gloucesters.

21st *Division*

Major-General D. G. M. Campbell.
G.S.O. 1. Lt.-Colonel H. E. Franklyn.

62nd *Infantry Brigade.*—Brig.-General G. H. Gater.
    12/13th Northumberland Fus.   1st Lincoln.
    2nd Lincoln.

64th Infantry Brigade.—Brig.-General H. R. Headlam.
    1st East Yorks. 9th K.O.Y.L.I. 15th D.L.I.
110th Infantry Brigade.—Brig.-General H. R. Cumming.
    6th Leicester. 7th Leicester. 8th Leicester.
Pioneers.—14th Northumberland Fus.

9th Division

Major-General C. A. Blacklock.[1]
G.S.O. 1. Lt.-Colonel T. C. Mudie.

26th Infantry Brigade.—Brig.-General J. Kennedy.
    8th Black Watch. 7th Seaforth Highs. 5th Cameron Highs.
27th Infantry Brigade.—Brig.-General W. D. Croft.
    11th Royal Scots. 12th Royal Scots. 6th K.O.S.B.
South African Brigade.—Brig.-General F. S. Dawson.
    1st South African. 2nd South African. 4th South African.
Pioneers.—9th Seaforth Highs.

[1] Brig.-General Tudor, C.R.A., commanded during the first days of the battle, as Major-General Blacklock was away on leave when the battle opened.

Divisions in G.H.Q. Reserve

20th Division

Major-General W. Douglas Smith.
G.S.O. 1. Lt.-Colonel J. McD. Haskard.

59th Infantry Brigade.—Brig.-General H. H. G. Hys-
lop.
    2nd Scottish Rifles. 11th K.R.R.C. 11th Rifle
    Brigade.
60th Infantry Brigade.—Brig.-General F. J. Duncan.
    6th K.S.L.I. 12th K.R.R.C. 12th Rifle Brig-
    ade.
61st Infantry Brigade.—Brig.-General J. K. Cochrane.
    12th King's (Liverpool). 7th Somerset L.I.
    7th D.C.L.I.
Pioneers.—11th D.L.I.

8th Division

Major-General W. C. G. Heneker.
G.S.O. 1. Lt.-Colonel C. C. Armitage.

23rd Infantry Brigade.—Brig.-General G. W. St. G.
Grogan, V.C.
    2nd Devon. 2nd West Yorks. 2nd Middlesex.
24th Infantry Brigade.—Brig.-General R. Haig.
    1st Worcester. 2nd Northampton. 1st Sher-
    wood Foresters.
25th Infantry Brigade.—Brig.-General C. Coffin, V.C.
    2nd R. Berks. 2nd East Lancs. 2nd Rifle
    Brigade.
Pioneers.—22nd D.L.I.

APPENDIX

50th *Division*

Brig.-General A. U. Stockley, officiating till 24.3.18,
replaced by
Major-General H. C. Jackson.
G.S.O. 1. Lt.-Colonel E. C. Anstey.

149*th Infantry Brigade.*—Brig.-General E. P. A.
Riddell.
    4th Northumberland Fus. 5th Northumberland
    Fus. 6th Northumberland Fus.
150*th Infantry Brigade.*—Brig.-General H. C. Rees.
    4th East Yorks. 4th Yorks. 5th Yorks.
151*st Infantry Brigade.*—Brig.-General C. T. Martin.
    5th D.L.I. 6th D.L.I. 8th D.L.I.
Pioneers.—7th D.L.I.

V Brigade R.F.C.

Brig.-General L. E. O. Charlton.

15*th (Corps) Wing.*—Lt.-Colonel I. A. E. Edwards.
    Nos. 8, 35, 52, 82, and 53 Squadrons.
22*nd (Army) Wing.*—Lt.-Colonel F. V. Holt.
    Nos. 23, 24, 54, 48, 84, 5 (Naval), and 101
    Squadrons.

INDEX

209

Date Due